# Contents

## Chapter 1: Abortion facts

## Chapter 2: Abortion debate

# Introduction

**Abortion** is Volume 302 in the **ISSUES** series. The aim of the series is to offer current, diverse information about important issues in our world, from a UK perspective.

## ABOUT ABORTION

Statistics show that the number of women undergoing abortions in England, Scotland and Wales is decreasing, and yet it remains a highly sensitive and much debated topic. This book explores the laws surrounding abortion procedure, both in the UK and globally. It considers the effects of having an abortion, physically and mentally, and goes on to look at arguments regarding abortion in Ireland, legal abortion until term and sex-selective abortions.

## OUR SOURCES

Titles in the **ISSUES** series are designed to function as educational resource books, providing a balanced overview of a specific subject.

The information in our books is comprised of facts, articles and opinions from many different sources, including:

⇨ Newspaper reports and opinion pieces

⇨ Website factsheets

⇨ Magazine and journal articles

⇨ Statistics and surveys

⇨ Government reports

⇨ Literature from special interest groups.

## A NOTE ON CRITICAL EVALUATION

Because the information reprinted here is from a number of different sources, readers should bear in mind the origin of the text and whether the source is likely to have a particular bias when presenting information (or when conducting their research). It is hoped that, as you read about the many aspects of the issues explored in this book, you will critically evaluate the information presented.

It is important that you decide whether you are being presented with facts or opinions. Does the writer give a biased or unbiased report? If an opinion is being expressed, do you agree with the writer? Is there potential bias to the 'facts' or statistics behind an article?

## ASSIGNMENTS

In the back of this book, you will find a selection of assignments designed to help you engage with the articles you have been reading and to explore your own opinions. Some tasks will take longer than others and there is a mixture of design, writing and research-based activities that you can complete alone or in a group.

## FURTHER RESEARCH

At the end of each article we have listed its source and a website that you can visit if you would like to conduct your own research. Please remember to critically evaluate any sources that you consult and consider whether the information you are viewing is accurate and unbiased.

## Useful weblinks

www.amnesty.org

www.bpas.org

www.care.org.uk

www.christianconcern.com

www.cmfblog.org.uk

www.theconversation.com

www.theguardian.com

www.healthcentre.org.uk

www.heraldscotland.com

www.huffingtonpost.co.uk

www.ibtimes.co.uk

www.mentalhealthy.co.uk

www.nhs.uk

www.nursingtimes.net

www.pregnancychoicesdirectory.com

www.pri.org

www.progressonline.org.uk

www.rcm.org.uk

researchbriefings.parliament.uk

www.telegraph.co.uk

# Statistics on abortion

## A note from the House of Commons Library.

This Note presents statistics on abortion in England & Wales, as well as Scotland. Numbers of abortions and rates per 1,000 women aged 15–44 are provided and a brief time series is presented. The period of gestation when the abortion took place is also considered as well as the method of abortion.

### Current legislation

Abortion is the commonly used term for the termination of an established pregnancy.

The Abortion Act 1967 came into effect on 27 April 1968, permitting abortion in Great Britain (not including Northern Ireland) by registered practitioners subject to certain conditions. Section 37 of the Human Fertilisation and Embryology Act (1990) made changes to the Abortion Act. It introduced a time limit of 24 weeks for grounds C and D. Grounds A, B and E are now without limit. Before this change, a 28- week limit had applied for all grounds.

### Grounds for permitting abortions under the current UK legislation

A legally induced abortion must be certified by two registered medical practitioners as justified under one or more of the following grounds:

A. The continuance of the pregnancy would involve risk to the life of the pregnant woman greater than if the pregnancy were terminated (Abortion Act, 1967 as amended, section 1(1)(c))

B. The termination is necessary to prevent grave permanent injury to the physical or mental health of the pregnant woman (section 1(1)(b)).

C. The pregnancy has not exceeded its 24th week and that the continuance of the pregnancy would involve risk, greater than if the pregnancy were terminated, of injury to the physical or mental health of the pregnant woman (section 1(1)(a)).

D. The pregnancy has not exceeded its 24th week and that the continuance of the pregnancy would involve risk, greater than if the pregnancy were terminated, of injury to the physical or mental health of any existing children of the family of the pregnant woman (section 1(1)(a)).

E. There is substantial risk that if the child were born it would suffer from such physical or mental abnormalities as to be seriously handicapped (section 1(1)(d)). Or in the case of an emergency, certified by the operating practitioner as immediately necessary:

F. To save the life of the pregnant woman (section 1(4)).

G. To prevent grave permanent injury to the physical or mental health of the pregnant woman (section 1(4)).

### Figures for England and Wales

There were 190,092 abortions notified as taking place in England and Wales in 2014. 0.4% fewer than in 2013.

Of these, 184,571 abortions were to residents of England and Wales, representing an age-standardised rate of 15.9 abortions per 1,000 resident women aged 15–44 years.

Over the past 50 years, the age standardised abortion rate increased from 10.8 in 1974 to a peak of 17.9 in 2007. The rate fell to 17.5 in 2008 and to 16.9 in 2009 where it remained before falling again over the past two years to the current rate of 15.9 in 2014.

### Age, marital status and ethnicity

The crude abortion rate in 2014 was highest at 28.0 per 1,000 for women aged 20–24. The under-16 abortion rate was 2.5 per 1,000 women and the under-18 rate was 11.1 per 1,000 women, both lower than in 2013. The rates for younger age groups in 2014 were lower than in 2013, most markedly for the under-18 age groups.

81% of abortions in 2014 were carried out for single women – of which 26% were single without a partner and 52% with a partner (3% did not state whether they had a partner), a proportion that has been rising from about two thirds since 1997.

The recording of ethnicity, as self-reported by the women involved, was introduced in 2002. In 2014, among women with ethnicity recorded, 77% of those having an abortion were White, 9% Asian or Asian British and 8% Black or Black British.

### Gestation period

The majority of abortions (92% in 2014) are performed at or under 13 weeks gestation. In 2014, 80% were at or under ten weeks and a further 12% at ten to 12 weeks. The proportion of abortions at under ten weeks has increased since 1997, and the proportion at over 13 weeks has reduced.

Abortions where gestation has exceeded its 20th week account for 2% of the total. There were 2,769 such abortions in 2014.

## Statutory grounds for abortion

The majority of abortions (98%) in 2014 were under ground C. The proportion of ground C abortions has risen steadily since 1997, with a corresponding reduction in ground D cases.

3,099 abortions (2%) were under ground E, risk that the child would be born handicapped. Congenital malformations were reported for 46% of cases under ground E and chromosomal abnormalities in 37%. Down's syndrome (21% of all ground E cases) was the most commonly reported chromosomal abnormality. Ground F or G abortions are rare.

## Location and funding

Treatment for the termination of pregnancy can only be carried out in an NHS hospital, NHS agencies (approved independent sector places under NHS contract) and approved places in the private sector. After 24 weeks, terminations can only be performed in an NHS hospital.

32% of abortions in 2014 were performed in NHS hospitals and 67% in NHS agencies, totalling 98% of abortions. The remaining 2% were privately funded. The proportion performed under NHS contract has been rising steadily since the early 1990s while the proportion of NHS hospital and private abortions has been falling.

## Method of abortion

Different methods exist to terminate a pregnancy, depending on the duration of gestation and personal circumstances of women involved. The main medical method involves the use of the abortifacient drug Mifegyne (Mifepristone, also known as RU486). The main surgical methods are vacuum aspiration (recommended at up to 15 weeks gestation) and dilatation and evacuation (D&E) (recommended where gestation is greater than 15 weeks).

Medical abortions accounted for 51% of the total in 2014. There has been a continuing upward trend in medical abortions since 1991 when Mifegyne was licensed for use in the UK. The proportion of medical abortions has more than doubled in the last five years.

Surgical abortions accounted for 49% of the total in 2014 and vacuum aspiration was used for 44% of these surgical abortions in 2014 and D&E alone in 4% of cases.

## Repeat abortions

37% of women undergoing abortions in 2014 had one or more previous abortions. The proportion has risen over the last decade from 32% in 2004.

Among women who had experienced a previous abortion 27% were under 25 and 46% were over 25.

Older women were more likely to have had a previous abortion: 47% of those aged 30–34 compared with 7% of those aged under 18.

### Figures for Scotland

There were 11,475 abortions performed in Scotland in 2014, the lowest reported since 1995.

The rate of terminations is highest among women aged 20–24 (18.9 per 1,000 women) and those aged 25–29 (15.1 per 1,000 women). Lower rates are seen in women aged 35–39 (6.7 per 1,000 women) and in women aged over 40 (2.3 per 1,000 women). For the first time between 2005 and 2014 the rate of terminations in the 25–29 age group in 2014 surpassed those in the 16–19 age group.

There is a clear link between abortion rate and levels of deprivation. The rate is 14.2 per 1,000 women in areas of high deprivation, compared to 8.2 per 1,000 women for the least deprived areas in Scotland.

The proportion of early terminations has been rising steadily in the last five years, with 80.5% of all terminations performed at less than ten weeks in 2014, compared to 76.1% in 2010. Only 0.5% of abortions were performed at 18 weeks or more.

The vast majority (98.5%) of terminations are undertaken under ground C.

*15 March 2016*

⇨ The above information is reprinted with kind permission from the Department of Health. Please visit researchbriefings. parliament.uk for further information.

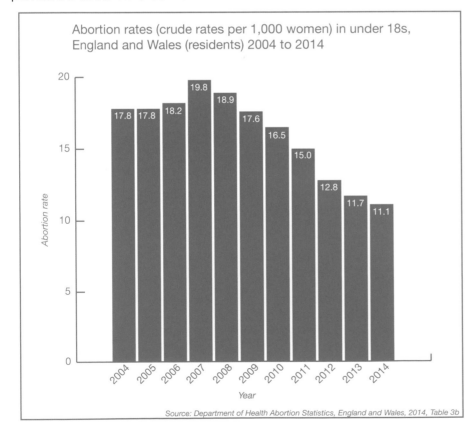

Abortion rates (crude rates per 1,000 women) in under 18s, England and Wales (residents) 2004 to 2014

Abortion rate — Year

2004: 17.8, 2005: 17.8, 2006: 18.2, 2007: 19.8, 2008: 18.9, 2009: 17.6, 2010: 16.5, 2011: 15.0, 2012: 12.8, 2013: 11.7, 2014: 11.1

*Source: Department of Health Abortion Statistics, England and Wales, 2014, Table 3b*

# I'm considering an abortion – what do I need to know?

## Abortion is the ending of pregnancy and it is available up to 24 weeks of pregnancy

Abortions take place in NHS hospitals or in private clinics.

In England, the majority of women can choose to have an abortion, which is funded by the NHS, either at an NHS hospital or at a private clinic. In Scotland, most abortions are carried out through the NHS in an NHS hospital.

If you are not sure about how many weeks pregnant you are, you may need to have an ultrasound scan and/or an internal examination.

There are two main methods of abortion: the medical and the surgical method.

### Early Medical Abortions (EMA) (up to nine weeks of pregnancy)

An early medical abortion (EMA) is one that can be carried out before nine weeks of pregnancy.

### How is an early medical abortion done?

This is a two-stage procedure, which involves separate visits to the unit.

⇨ For the first part of your treatment you will be given a tablet called Mifepristone. This drug can make some people feel sick.

⇨ For the second part of your treatment you will be given more medicine, a drug called Prostaglandin. This will cause the womb to contract and expel the pregnancy. You will be given painkillers for stomach cramp and some anti-sickness medication to take if necessary. At this stage you will be observed for a period of time and then may be allowed home. The pregnancy will be passed over a period of one to six hours. In some clinics or hospitals you are required to stay until the procedure is complete.

⇨ You will need a follow-up visit if you go home to complete the abortion. This is to ensure that the medication has worked.

⇨ Sometimes, the EMA medication does not work. In this case a surgical abortion would be offered.

A list of any medical conditions that you may have will be taken by the clinic or hospital to make sure the medicines used in this type of abortion are suitable for you.

### Surgical abortion or vacuum (suction) termination (from seven to 15 weeks of pregnancy)

Vacuum aspiration, or suction termination, is a procedure that uses gentle suction to remove the pregnancy from the womb. The procedure usually takes five to ten minutes and can be carried out under a local anaesthetic (where the area is numbed) or general anaesthetic (where you are put to sleep).

To soften the cervix (the entrance of the womb) and make it easier to open, a tablet may be placed in the vagina a few hours before the abortion.

After this type of abortion, you will usually be able to go home the same day. However, following the procedure you may bleed a little for up to 14 days.

### Late medical abortion (from 13 weeks of pregnancy)

As well as being used for early abortion, the same medicines can be used for abortion later in pregnancy. However, the abortion will take longer, and more than one dose of medicine may be needed.

After the procedure, you can return home the same day, but sometimes an overnight stay in hospital is required.

### Surgical dilation and evacuation (from 15 weeks of pregnancy)

Surgical dilation and evacuation (D&E) is a procedure that is carried out under general anaesthetic.

The cervix is gently stretched and dilated (opened) and the pregnancy removed.

The procedure usually takes 10-20 minutes to perform and you may be able to return home the same day. You may have some bleeding for up to 14 days.

### Late abortion (20–24 weeks)

There are two options for a late abortion carried out at 20–24 weeks. Both require an overnight stay in hospital.

⇨ Surgical abortion

⇨ Medically induced abortion

### Risks of an abortion

Abortion poses few risks to a woman's physical health, particularly when carried out during the first 12 weeks of pregnancy.

### Risks at the time of an abortion

The risk of problems occurring during an abortion is low. However, there are more likely to be problems if an abortion is carried out later in a pregnancy.

### Risks after an abortion

After an abortion, the main risk is infection in the womb. This happens if traces of the pregnancy have not been removed. If you have an infection after an abortion, you may bleed heavily from your vagina and have some period-like pain. Antibiotics are usually used to treat the infection. Repeated abortions can cause damage to the entrance of the womb (cervix). After an abortion, you may have some period-type pains, and some vaginal bleeding, which should gradually lessen after a few days. Most women can return to their usual activities within a day or so. However, seek medical attention if you have severe pain or if bleeding has not stopped after 14 days.

### Mixed emotions

Some women will also have an emotional response following abortion. Sometimes a mixture of positive and negative reactions is experienced. For example:

Positive reactions:

⇨ Relief

⇨ Happiness.

Negative reactions:

⇨ Sorrow

⇨ Sadness

⇨ Guilt

⇨ Regret

⇨ Grief

⇨ Loss.

In some women these negative reactions can lead to:

⇨ Depression

⇨ Anxiety

⇨ Low self-worth.

Women vary greatly in their emotional responses when considering abortion. To make a fully informed decision it may well be helpful for you to have the opportunity to look at all the options and possible outcomes.

Your may feel that your circumstances affect your freedom to make a decision.

CareConfidential offers a safe place to consider and discuss all your options.

A CareConfidential telephone advisor is available on our national helpline 0300 4000 999 or use our free CareConfidential Online Advisor service.

You may also like to:

⇨ Make an appointment with your GP to discuss abortion options with them.

You may be able to refer yourself to an abortion provider, without seeing your GP, if you prefer:

⇨ Visit your Sexual Health Clinic

⇨ Contact the British Pregnancy Advisory Service

⇨ Contact Marie Stopes International.

You will be able to discuss abortion options with all of these abortion providers.

⇨ The above information is reprinted with kind permission from the Pregnancy Choices Directory. Please visit www. pregnancychoicesdirectory. com for further information.

# Abortion: where to go

**If you're pregnant and considering an abortion, find out who to talk to and where and when an abortion can take place.**

If you're not sure whether you're pregnant, find out about doing a pregnancy test.

### How do I get an abortion?

You need to be referred by a doctor to get an abortion on the NHS. There are usually three stages to the referral process.

First, visit a GP or contraception clinic. They can refer you to NHS abortion services and discuss your options with you. If you're under 25, you can also go to a young people's service such as Brook.

The next stage is an assessment appointment at the clinic or hospital where the abortion will be carried out. At this appointment, the doctor or nurse will explain the different types of abortion and will be able to talk things over with you if you wish.

Finally, you will be given another appointment at the hospital or clinic to have the abortion.

Alternatively, you can go directly to an independent abortion provider

such as bpas (the British Pregnancy Advisory Service) or Marie Stopes UK, which can provide abortions on the NHS as well as private abortions that you pay for.

You can find your nearest contraceptive clinic or genito-urinary medicine (GUM) clinic by using the sexual health service search. Or you can look in your local phone directory or on the FPA website. Young people can visit the Brook website to find their nearest Brook centre.

You can also pay for an abortion at a private clinic. The cost (around £400 or more) depends on how far along the pregnancy you are and the type of abortion you're having. You can contact a private clinic without seeing a GP, and you can find one through organisations such as:

⇨ FPA

⇨ bpas

⇨ Marie Stopes UK

⇨ local sexual health services

### How late into the pregnancy can I have an abortion?

Abortion is legal in Great Britain at any time up to 24 weeks of pregnancy. The majority of abortions are carried out before 13 weeks, and most of the rest before 20 weeks.

There are some exceptions. If the mother's life is at risk, or if the child would be born with a severe physical or mental disability, an abortion may be carried out after 24 weeks.

### What are my options?

It largely depends on how far into the pregnancy you are. A doctor can talk you through the different methods available.

The Royal College of Obstetricians and Gynaecologists (RCOG) has a leaflet called *Abortion care* (PDF, 217kb), which contains a useful timeline on page 4 showing the types of abortion that can be carried out at different stages of pregnancy.

### How long will I have to wait?

Waiting times vary around the country, but, as a rule, you should not have to wait for more than two weeks from your initial appointment to having an abortion.

### Can I be refused an abortion?

It's rare for anyone to be refused an abortion. A doctor may have moral objections to abortion, but if that's the case they should refer you to another doctor or nurse who can help. It can be difficult to get later abortions, so the earlier you seek help the better.

By law, two doctors have to agree that you can have an abortion. Usually this is the first doctor you see and a second doctor who will perform the abortion, or one who works at the contraceptive clinic or hospital.

### Will it be confidential?

Yes, all information is kept confidential and nobody else will know about it, not even your partner or parents. You can also ask the hospital or clinic not to inform your GP.

If you are under 16, your doctor does not have to mention it to your parents. He or she will encourage you to involve your parents or another supportive adult, but you don't have to so long as the doctor believes that you're competent and can make the decision yourself.

### Can I choose where to have an abortion?

Yes. You can ask to have the abortion somewhere other than your local clinic or hospital if you wish.

### Can I get any counselling before or afterwards?

Most abortion services offer counselling if you feel you need help with any worries or feelings you're having. It's normal to experience a range of emotions after an abortion, such as relief, sadness, happiness or feelings of loss.

Each woman's response is unique. To find out what support is available in your area, ask your GP or a doctor or nurse at your contraception clinic.

### Will having an abortion affect my chances of having a baby in the future?

If there were no problems with the abortion, such as infection, then it will not affect your changes of becoming pregnant in the future, although you may have a slightly higher risk of premature birth.

*5 November 2014*

⇨ The above information is reprinted with kind permission from NHS Choices. Please visit www.nhs.uk for further information.

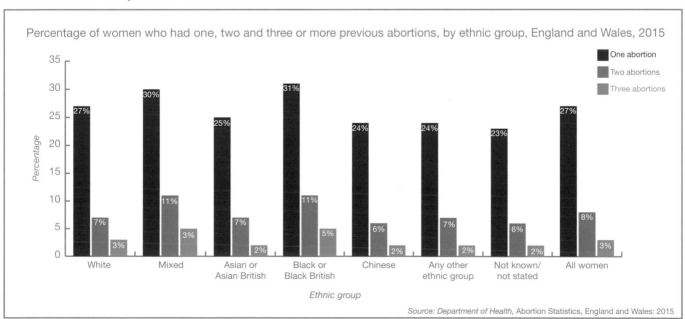

Percentage of women who had one, two and three or more previous abortions, by ethnic group, England and Wales, 2015

Source: Department of Health, Abortion Statistics, England and Wales: 2015

# Abortion: what happens

**If you've decided to have an abortion, here's what you can expect.**

If you are unable or do not wish to continue with a pregnancy, your GP or a doctor at a sexual health clinic will refer you to a clinic or hospital for an assessment. This is also where an abortion can take place. In some areas, you can go straight to an independent abortion clinic without being referred.

**"If you are unable or do not wish to continue with a pregnancy, your GP or a doctor at a sexual health clinic will refer you to a clinic or hospital for an assessment"**

### Your medical assessment before abortion

The assessment will be the same if you go directly to an independent provider (such as the British Pregnancy Advisory Service (bpas) or Marie Stopes) without going to your GP.

During the assessment you:

⇨ can discuss your reasons for requesting an abortion and how certain you are of that decision

⇨ should be offered the chance to discuss your situation with a counsellor

⇨ can talk to a nurse or doctor about the abortion methods that are available

⇨ can discuss contraceptive options to prevent a further unplanned pregnancy

⇨ might be tested for sexually transmitted infections (STIs) and anaemia (low iron levels)

⇨ might be given an ultrasound scan if there's doubt about how many weeks pregnant you are.

Independent providers, such as Marie Stopes and bpas, have useful information on the consultation or assessment, counselling, and medical and surgical abortion.

### Will I have to stay in hospital after an abortion?

It depends how many weeks pregnant you are and which abortion method is being used. Normally, you can go home the same day. If the abortion takes place after 20 weeks, you'll usually have to stay overnight.

### What happens during an abortion?

There are different kinds of abortion, depending on how many weeks pregnant you are. An abortion service should be able to offer you a choice of different kinds of abortion, but this may not always be possible.

#### Medical abortion

A medical abortion involves taking medication to end the pregnancy. It doesn't require surgery or an anaesthetic, and can be used at any stage of pregnancy.

If you have a medical abortion, the first drug you take is Mifepristone. This stops the production of hormones that allow the pregnancy to continue.

Up to two days later, you will have another appointment where you take a second drug called Prostaglandin. This will either be a tablet you take by mouth, or a pessary put inside your vagina. Prostaglandin causes the lining of the uterus (womb) to break down. This causes bleeding and loss of the pregnancy about four to six hours later. You may have to stay at the clinic while this happens.

Medical abortion carried out up to nine weeks of pregnancy is known as early medical abortion. If a medical abortion is carried out after nine weeks, you may need a second dose of Prostaglandin. If you have a medical abortion between 13 and 24 weeks of pregnancy, you will usually need to be in hospital or the clinic.

#### Surgical abortion

Surgical abortion involves having a procedure under a local or general anaesthetic. There are two methods of surgical abortion:

In some parts of the World unsafe abortion is the only choice.

Suction aspiration can be used from seven to 15 weeks of pregnancy. It involves inserting a tube through the vagina and into the uterus, and removing the pregnancy using suction. It's usually carried out under local anaesthetic, which is injected into the cervix. Most women go home a few hours later.

Dilation and evacuation (D&E) is used after around 15 weeks of pregnancy. The cervix is gently stretched and dilated to enable special forceps to be inserted. Suction is then used to remove the pregnancy. It usually takes between 10 and 20 minutes to perform D&E under general anaesthetic (you'll be asleep while it happens). If there are no complications, you can usually go home that same day.

### Does having an abortion hurt?

You'll have some period-type pain or discomfort. The later the abortion, the more painful it may be. You'll be advised about taking appropriate painkillers.

With suction abortions, the injection to numb the cervix can sometimes be painful.

You might experience some bleeding and period-type pains for up to 14 days after any type of abortion.

### Are there any risks from abortion?

The earlier an abortion is carried out, the lower the risks. The main risk after an abortion is infection in the womb, so you may be given antibiotics. In rare cases, the uterus may perforate (this means it might tear).

The risks associated with abortion are:

⇨ damage to the uterus – happens in less than one in 1,000 medical abortions performed between 12 and 24 weeks, and up to four in 1,000 surgical abortions

⇨ damage to the cervix – happens in no more than ten in every 1,000 abortions

⇨ haemorrhage (excessive bleeding) – happens in about one in every 1,000 abortions.

You should go back to your doctor or clinic immediately if you get symptoms of an infection after an abortion. Symptoms include:

⇨ high temperature

⇨ vaginal discharge

⇨ abdominal pain that doesn't improve after taking painkillers.

If you have signs of still being pregnant after the abortion, you should have another pregnancy test. If it's positive, you'll need a scan to confirm that the abortion hasn't worked. The abortion procedure may need to be carried out again.

### Will an abortion affect my ability to have a baby in the future?

There is no evidence linking a previous abortion with future pregnancy problems. However, the Royal College of Obstetricians and Gynaecologists (RCOG) states that if you have a number of late-term abortions, there might be a higher risk of miscarriage or early birth.

### Could I get pregnant again immediately after an abortion?

Yes. Some women can get pregnant within four weeks of having an abortion. You will be given advice about contraception at the time of your abortion and offered to have your chosen method supplied or fitted immediately, so that you are able to plan any future pregnancy.

*30 November 2017*

⇨ The above information is reprinted with kind permission from NHS Choices. Please visit www.nhs.uk for further information.

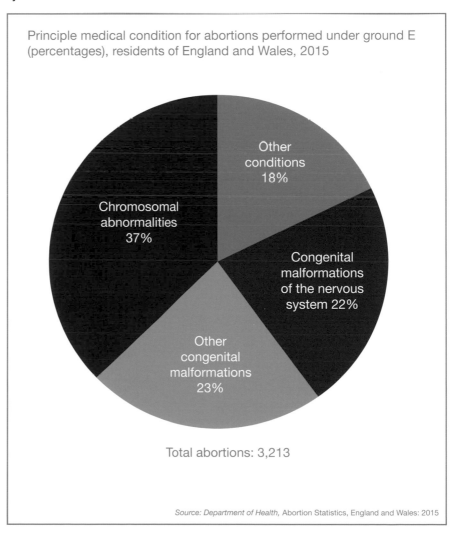

Principle medical condition for abortions performed under ground E (percentages), residents of England and Wales, 2015

Other conditions 18%

Chromosomal abnormalities 37%

Congenital malformations of the nervous system 22%

Other congenital malformations 23%

Total abortions: 3,213

*Source: Department of Health, Abortion Statistics, England and Wales: 2015*

# Growing pro-life movement presents a challenge to defenders of abortion rights

**An article from The Conversation.**

*By Graeme Hayes, Reader in Political Sociology, Aston University,*
*Pam Lowe Senior Lecturer in Sociology, Aston University and*
*Sarah-Jane Page Lecturer in Sociology, Aston University*

**THE CONVERSATION**

Birmingham hosted the fourth annual March for Life, bringing together 'pro-life' campaigners from across the UK (and further afield, including Ireland, France, Spain, Mexico, Slovakia).

The event was much bigger than last year. We counted around 1,000 participants in all, double the number attending in 2015. And this was a much slicker operation than what has been seen before.

Crash barriers and professional security cordoned off space in Victoria Square. Entrance was controlled by the organisers and the speakers and musicians had a professional PA, stage and big screen. There were even merchandise stalls and face-painting.

The event marketing seemed designed to appeal especially to a youth demographic. We saw the slogan "Life from Conception, No Exception!" printed on wristbands, hoodies and t-shirts. One participant told us: "It's got a kind of a Glastonbury feel about it!"

Last year, it took just a line of police to separate marchers from abortion rights campaigners, who were able to disrupt the closing rally, drowning out the PA system.

### Changing approach

On this evidence, the anti-abortion movement, if still very small, is growing in mainland Britain.

But that growth could cause dilemmas. The marchers seemed united against abortion but less in agreement about what should actually be done about it.

Some argued: "We're not here to change the law, we're here to save lives," while others spoke of closing down "the abortion industry".

For some, pro-life activism is a personal commitment to make a difference as an individual, offering what they see as support to other women, through and after pregnancy. Others told us that getting an abortion in Britain is currently "too easy". The wish to provide support is very different from making it harder for women to get an abortion by changing the law.

> ## "We're not here to change the law, we're here to save lives"

Every participant we spoke to defined abortion as the murder of human life (several told us their belief that life begins at conception was supported by science). But again, they struggled to reach a definitive conclusion on how this should be handled.

One student activist suggested abortion should be considered infanticide before backtracking and agreeing that women should not be prosecuted for having an abortion. This may be only a personal view but it points to an absent common position on how women who have abortions should be treated.

How to represent abortion at events of this kind is another crucial issue. Last year, organisers stressed that participants should not display graphic images of aborted foetuses. This year, the official position was left unspoken, publicly, at least.

The question is important if the march is to bring together activists from often diverse groups. Abort67 – which has courted controversy for its use of

graphic images – ran a stall at this year's event; but, unusually, did not openly display its signs. The march's official signs carried slogans, whilst banners showed images of babies. The event avoided the issue by not representing abortion in images at all.

Familiar Catholic iconography was on display, including a Cross of Life, where participants could place prayers, and a Mercy Bus – a sort of mobile confession box.

But we saw more secular elements being woven into proceedings this year. Ryan Bomberger, of the pro-life Radiance Foundation, claimed abortion is "the social injustice of the day" because it implies that "somehow, some lives are more equal than others".

Bomberger even co-opted celebrity, encouraging demonstrators to wave their iPhones in the air. The logic here seemed to be that Apple founder Steve Jobs, like Bomberger, had been adopted – proving that great opportunities can be missed because of abortion.

Following the march, Canadian pro-life activist Stephanie Gray gave a contrasting talk. Where Bomberger was upbeat and motivational, Gray was careworn and emotional as she described a "broken culture".

She said we must "learn how to weep for the 200,000 little children who die every year in the UK". Asking the crowd to treat activism as a daily event, Gray steeped her talk in messages of good and evil, and the need to pray for abortionists' souls, as they have "followed the father of lies and the prince of darkness".

The event culminated with a vigil led by one of three Bishops, who offered prayers to all constituents in the abortion debate, from pregnant mothers to medical practitioners, and a minute's silence "to pray for the victims of abortion".

### A changing response

The changing nature of this march over the years, particularly in terms of scale, reveals subtle shifts in its ambitions and its target audience. By bringing in secular elements and branding, it is clearly trying to appeal beyond its core supporters, into the wider public.

> **"it looks like the anti-abortion movement remains some way from its goal of appealing beyond a limited strain of committed Catholicism"**

But from our observations, it looks like the anti abortion movement remains some way from its goal of appealing beyond a limited strain of committed Catholicism.

There is also still a reliance on speakers from North America and Africa, where the anti-abortion movement is more developed. This is perhaps a reminder that it has had a harder time gaining traction in Britain's broadly liberal secular landscape.

That said, it's clear that the event's increased professionalism also poses questions for abortion rights activists in the UK. Faced with an evolving British pro-life movement, they will have to think carefully about how to react, and how to defend access to abortion in Britain.

*16 May 2016*

⇨ The above information is reprinted with kind permission from *The Conversation*. Please visit www.theconversation.com for further information.

# England and Wales abortion rate is stable, more than half of women ending pregnancies are already mothers

The abortion rate for England and Wales was 15.9 per 1,000 women aged 15–44 in 2014. Rates fell slightly among all age groups under 25, and remained stable or rose marginally among women over 25. 56% of abortions in England and Wales were performed on women over the age of 25 in 2014.

More than half (54%) of women ending pregnancies had already given birth, up from 47% a decade ago.

The vast majority of abortions are performed at under 13 weeks (92% in 2014), with a continuing increase in the proportion carried out under ten weeks. Access to Early Medical Abortion, where pills are taken to induce a miscarriage, has played an important role in the numbers of women able to access early procedures. A small number of women will need access to services after 20 weeks (2%) due to later detection of pregnancy, dramatic changes in personal circumstances, or because a problem has been diagnosed with a wanted pregnancy.

The repeat abortion rate remains stable, with 37% of all abortions provided to women who have had a previous procedure. This rate is in keeping with those in comparable developed countries such as France and Sweden. Given that women are fertile for more than 30 years, it is unsurprising that women may experience an unplanned pregnancy or a pregnancy they cannot carry to term on more than one occasion.

Much work has been done to improve contraceptive services for younger women, and it is important to ensure older women have the same access to convenient, high-quality services. The British Pregnancy Advisory Services believes more in particular could be done to support women's contraceptive needs in the postnatal period, as we regularly see women experiencing unwanted pregnancy in the period after giving birth.

bpas chief executive Ann Furedi said:

"No form of contraception is 100% effective, and women will always need straightforward access to abortion services as a back-up if they are to plan their lives and families in the way they see fit. Having done so much to improve contraceptive services for younger women, we must also ensure the needs of older women are met.

"One in three women will have an abortion in her lifetime. It is a fundamental part of women's reproductive healthcare, as these statistics demonstrate. It makes no sense that abortion remains within the criminal law in this country, and that women still the need authorisation of two doctors before they can end their own pregnancy. It also remains a travesty that in 2015, women from Northern Ireland are unable to access the care they need at home. The time really has come to decriminalise abortion across the UK and regulate it like every other women's healthcare procedure."

*9 June 2015*

⇨ The above information is reprinted with kind permission from bpas. Please visit www.bpas.org for further information.

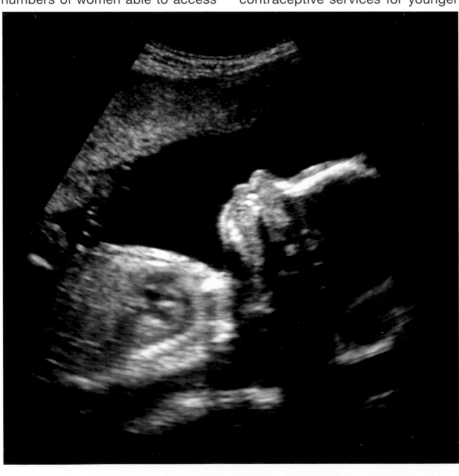

# Britain's real abortion scandal is how hard it is for some women to have one

*By Verity Ryan*

Is abortion legal in the UK? Chances are, you just thought to yourself, "yes": Britain is a liberal society, with progressive attitudes towards women; free healthcare; and, most important here, the 1967 Abortion Act.

You might be surprised to find then that the answer is actually "No". Abortions are illegal, bar a few allowable exceptions. What is more, application of these exceptions is not consistently applied across the UK. In short, if you find yourself in need of an abortion, pray you have the right postcode.

The Abortion Act does not apply to Northern Ireland. In recent weeks there has been a steady stream of coverage about women who have been prosecuted for obtaining illegal terminations. One recent case concerns a woman facing criminal charges and a possible life sentence over allegations she helped her daughter have an abortion.

Barriers to abortion services are lower in the rest of the UK, but they still exist.

The NHS England website itself states that NHS funding of abortion services can vary from 60 per cent to 90 per cent of local demand; waiting times also vary. In 2014, nearly 4,000 abortions were conducted in private clinics, with costs ranging from £600 to over £2,000.

Most startling however are the informal barriers to access faced by women in Scotland compared to those in England and Wales.

Broadly speaking, the Abortion Act permits terminations if gestation is under 24 weeks, and two doctors judge that continuation of the pregnancy will damage the physical or mental health of the woman in question, or other children they have. Whilst the Act applies to England, Wales and Scotland (Northern Ireland is still governed by legislation from 1861), investigations by an Edinburgh University academic, Carrie Purcell, suggest that after 18 weeks, abortion for non-medical purposes are rarely provided in Scotland – effectively the time limit for termination in Scotland is 6 weeks below the official legal limit.

A lack of equipment for later abortions is one reason given for this. Perhaps more damming though is evidence that some GPs are misinformed about the law – one GP in Purcell's study told a woman who was 17 weeks pregnant that she

## What is the law in Northern Ireland?

It is unlawful to perform an abortion, except to preserve the life or mental health of the mother, and anyone who performs the procedure faces life imprisonment.

## What about the 1967 Abortion Act?

It applies everywhere in the UK, except Northern Ireland.

## Can women have abortions on the NHS?

Even if they travel to England, they have to pay for it privately. In the last five years, 24,599 women travelled from the north and south of Ireland, where abortion is also banned, to England or Wales for terminations.

## Is Northern Ireland's law about to change?

The Northern Ireland Human Rights Commission (NIHRC) took a case against the Department of Justice, to try and change the law to offer women and girls a choice of accessing a termination in circumstances of fatal foetal abnormality, rape or incest.

## What does the judge's ruling mean?

The judge agreed with the NIHRC that the current law is incompatible with human rights law and results in a breach of the rights of women and girls seeking a termination of pregnancy in these circumstances. But he said it was up to Stormont to change it.

## Could there be an appeal?

All parties in the case – the NIHRC and the Department of Justice – have six weeks to appeal after the judgement is delivered in December.

was too late for an abortion as the foetus was "a baby now". Perhaps that was simple ignorance of the law, but the suspicion remains that some health professionals find the procedures distasteful and do not support them.

This is not the first time that that the influence of personal views on abortion provision in Scotland has been highlighted: in 2014 two Catholic midwives in Glasgow brought a legal challenge over whether they could be required to support staff who were involved in carrying out terminations. Their case was upheld in the Court of Session, but later rejected by the Supreme Court.

Next year will mark 50 years since the passage of the Abortion Act. The law was meant to end the deaths and damage resulting from desperate, backstreet abortions. Whilst the era of botched, amateur terminations is gone, official barriers in Northern Ireland and unofficial barriers for some women in Scotland, mean many still face the decision of whether to continue with an unwanted pregnancy, procure an abortion illegally – at greater personal risk – or get together the substantial funds and emotional grit required to travel away from home to access one safely.

So will equality of access be any better over the next 50 years? Current developments suggest not: devolution of powers over abortion, powerful anti-abortion lobbies in Northern Ireland and Scotland, and mixed beliefs at the top of politics suggests that divergence, rather than convergence, will be the tale of decades to come.

An amendment to the Scotland Bill means Holyrood will be able to legislate on abortion rights and whilst Nicola Sturgeon has made it clear that she has no intentions to change the law, not all of her SNP colleagues will agree – notably ex-health secretary, Alex Neil, has in the past been reported as favouring a reduction in the 24 weeks time limit.

Political sentiment can change, particularly when key voters are at stake. A healthy slice of SNP gains came from Roman Catholics, once a reliable bastion of support for Labour. In light of new Holyrood powers the Catholic Church in Scotland is now mobilising around the abortion issue: recently a letter was read out in Scottish Catholic churches urging parishioners to join a political party and bring to the upcoming Scottish elections "the benefits of insight [their] Christian faith gives".

Only time will tell how much pressure the church and its flock will exert on abortion legislation but it is safe to say that the Catholic vote remains an important one in Scotland, and the anti-abortion lobby is alive and well north of the border.

Unwanted pregnancies happen to women all over the world – from the favelas of Brazil, to the affluent high rises of Hong Kong; from the villages of Scotland to the market towns of middle England. Need does not disappear as geography changes but the personal costs do – whether it be health, financial or social.

Should we accept this variation within the borders of the UK, or should women living here be accorded the dignity of safe and equal access wherever they live? Let's hope it doesn't take until 2067 to get a positive answer to that.

*5 May 2016*

⇨ The above information is reprinted with kind permission from *The Telegraph*. Please visit www.telegraph.co.uk for further information.

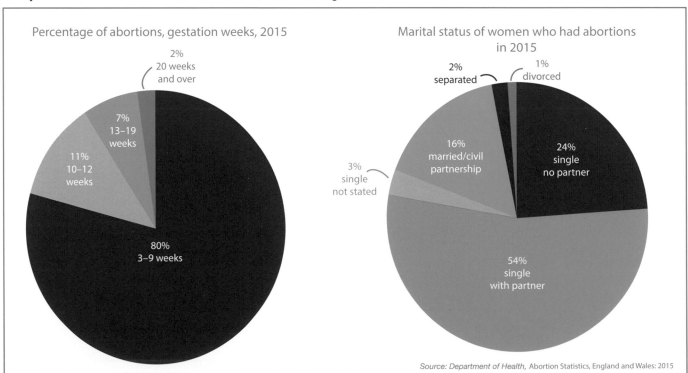

Percentage of abortions, gestation weeks, 2015

- 2% 20 weeks and over
- 7% 13–19 weeks
- 11% 10–12 weeks
- 80% 3–9 weeks

Marital status of women who had abortions in 2015

- 2% separated
- 1% divorced
- 16% married/civil partnership
- 3% single not stated
- 24% single no partner
- 54% single with partner

*Source: Department of Health, Abortion Statistics, England and Wales: 2015*

# Abortion is still illegal in the UK, thanks to this Victorian law

**THE CONVERSATION**

*An article from* **The Conversation.**

*By Sally Sheldon, Professor of Law, Kent Law School, University of Kent*

You probably know that abortion services are available in Britain on the National Health Service. What you may not know is that abortion is still potentially punishable by life imprisonment. That includes terminations very early in a pregnancy.

Abortion is still a criminal offence in the UK under the Offences Against the Person Act 1861. It is legal only when carried out under conditions of strict medical control.

As things stand, a terrified teenager, who takes abortion drugs that she has bought over the Internet rather than tell anyone that she is pregnant, is committing a crime that is punishable by life imprisonment.

The 1861 act is an archaic, badly flawed piece of legislation, which is ripe for reform. It includes specific offences such as failing to feed one's servants properly.

The act is so widely recognised as out of date that the Law Commission is conducting a major review of its content. Yet this review does not include those sections of the act that deal with abortion.

## Victorian rules

The 1861 act is grounded in the moral concerns and medical realities of mid-Victorian Britain. It was the product of an all-male parliament and was passed almost 60 years before the first women won the right to vote. This was a time when the mere fact of publishing a book on contraception was reason enough for a woman to be deemed morally unsuitable as a mother and to have her child removed from her care.

The effects of this harsh, punitive statute have been mitigated by legislation introduced in 1967, which permits abortions under medical control, but this second law is out of date too. It imposes a range of clinically unjustifiable restrictions on women seeking an abortion – most notably by requiring two doctors, rather than the pregnant woman herself, to decide if an abortion is justified. It also fails to offer any protection to the terrified teenager described above.

It is true that women are seldom charged for getting an abortion – but the fact that an archaic law is not enforced is not justification for retaining it.

## Time for change

It is high time abortion was decriminalised in the UK. That would not leave abortion services unregulated. Non-consensual, dangerous or negligent practice would be caught by the same mass of criminal, civil, administrative and disciplinary provisions that regulate other areas of medical practice.

But it would mean recognising that the threat of prison is no fit response to the pregnant teenager above or, indeed, to any woman who feels unable to access formal healthcare services. Neither are these provisions the best way of policing the boundaries of acceptable medical practice.

Sweeping away criminal prohibitions on abortion would also begin to address the stigma associated with a procedure sought by one in three British women at some point in their lives, and the health professionals that care for them.

It would offer the chance to remove clinically unnecessary barriers to the provision of high-quality, compassionate services. It would address the curious legal anomaly that requires doctors in all contexts save for this one, to recognise that patients are adults, capable of "accepting responsibility for the taking of risks affecting their own lives, and living with the consequences of their choices".

Removing criminal prohibitions on abortion would undoubtedly be fiercely opposed by those who believe that the embryo or foetus is a full moral person, of equal worth to the woman who carries it. But very few modern Britons (including those who identify as Christian) appear to take this extreme view. And while the moral beliefs of the minority should be respected in making decisions about their own healthcare, they should not dictate the shape of services for the majority.

Today, 92% of abortions are performed in the first 12 weeks of pregnancy. Most British people believe that, at least in these very early stages, it is up to the woman to decide whether or not to continue a pregnancy. Most also believe that the Government has no business interfering with that right.

For many of us, this is not because we believe that the growing, human foetus has no moral significance. It is because we trust women to make morally significant decisions. And we understand that women cannot participate equally in society unless we have the fundamental right to control our own fertility.

The onus should be on those who wish to retain the threat of a prison sentence to explain why criminal sanction offers a useful and appropriate part of a modern response to addressing the problem of unwanted pregnancy.

It is almost 100 years since the British Parliament recognised that women should have the right to vote. Now it should recognise that they should equally have the right to make fundamental decisions about their own fertility.

*6 October 2015*

⇨ The above information is reprinted with kind permission from *The Conversation*. Please visit www.theconversation.com for further information.

# Abortion laws around the world: from bans to easy access

**Religion and culture help determine the rules, which range from tight restrictions to terminations virtually on demand until the point of viability.**

*By Pamela Duncan, Molly Redden in New York and Jonathan Watts in Rio de Janeiro*

It is easier for a woman to get an abortion in conservative US states like Texas, Catholic European countries like Poland and Portugal – and even in parts of Latin America – than it is in Northern Ireland.

Abortion laws in Northern Ireland and the Irish Republic are the most restrictive in Europe. Terminations in both jurisdictions are only permissible on the grounds of a threat to the life of the mother.

In most other parts of Europe abortion is allowed without restriction up to between ten and 14 weeks' gestation. In most countries abortions can be carried out beyond this point, but only on specific grounds.

So, for example, in Greece abortions can be carried out on demand up to a limit of 12 weeks. However, a limit of 19 weeks applies in cases where the pregnancy was the result of rape and 24 weeks where there is a threat to the life or health of the woman and in cases of foetal abnormality that would result in a serious congenital defect.

An exception to these graduated restrictions on abortion is The Netherlands where, the United Nations notes, "abortion is permitted virtually on request at any time between implantation and viability if performed by a physician in a (licensed) hospital or clinic".

In Poland, abortion is legal in certain circumstances, including where the pregnancy is the result of rape or incest, in cases of foetal impairment or to avert a danger to the health or life of the pregnant woman. The country has the lowest recorded abortion rate in Europe at just two abortions per 1,000 live births in 2012.

In Finland, Iceland and the UK restrictions are in place yet abortion rates remain relatively high at 174, 223 and 253 terminations per 1,000 live births.

In Catholic Portugal and Spain abortion on demand was introduced as a result of a 2007 referendum in the former and a 2010 law change in the latter.

However, in both countries it remains contentious. In Portugal, a recently adopted bill requires women to pay for terminations and to undergo more stringent tests beforehand. In Spain in 2014, the Government had to abandon its plans to enact legislation that would have imposed some of the tightest restrictions in Europe.

By far the highest abortion rate recorded in Europe is in Russia, where 551 abortions were recorded per 1,000 live births in 2011 according to figures compiled by the World Health Organization.

### The Americas

In the US, where abortion laws vary from state to state, the Centers for Disease Control and Prevention reported 210 abortions per 1,000 live births in 2012.

States cannot pass laws banning abortion outright and

I'D LIKE TO TALK TO SOMEONE ABOUT AN ABORTION...

– WHICH COUNTRY ARE YOU IN?

so they impose restrictions, such as waiting periods, to delay women, along with onerous requirements that cause abortion clinics to shut down. Limited access to providers can amount to a de facto ban on abortion.

A law in Texas is a good case in point. The law, now being debated before the US Supreme Court, may close half of all the state's abortion clinics. Before the law, which the state's Republican legislature passed in 2013, Texas had 41 clinics. Today, the number has dwindled to 20. If the law is fully upheld, only nine or ten clinics will remain.

More than 5.4 million women of reproductive age live in Texas. If only a few abortion providers were left, some researchers estimate that nearly two million women would live more than 50 miles from the nearest abortion clinic. But even with 20 abortion clinics up and running, it is already nearly impossible for many women to have an abortion. In Dallas, Forth Worth and Austin, women are waiting up to 20 days to be seen by a doctor, at which point the procedure becomes more expensive.

The law is also confusing: abortion providers and pro-choice nonprofit-making organisations have reported getting phone calls from many women wanting to know if abortion is still legal in Texas.

And there is emerging evidence that the law is dangerous. One survey found that between 100,000 and 240,000 women in Texas have tried to perform their own abortions at home with pills or sharp objects.

## Latin America

As the most secular and social progressive nation in South America, Uruguay has blazed the trail towards abortion decriminalisation in this predominantly Catholic continent.

After a 25-year campaign by feminist groups, parliament gave its approval in 2012 for terminations of pregnancies up to 12 weeks regardless of circumstances, and up to 14 weeks in cases of alleged rape.

The only restriction is that women seeking such a procedure must first discuss the matter with a panel of at least three professionals, including a gynaecologist, a mental health professional and a social worker. After they explain the risks and alternatives, she must then wait for a five-day 'reflection period' before deciding whether to go ahead.

Almost one in ten chose to continue their pregnancies, but abortions are becoming more common. In 2014, 12 out of every 1,000 women aged between 15 and 45 had an abortion. This was about 20% more than in the previous year.

This contrasts sharply with most other nations in Latin America. In El Salvador, anti-abortion laws are so strict that some women have been jailed for having a miscarriage. In Paraguay, an 11-year-old girl who was allegedly raped by her stepfather was forced to give birth against her wishes.

Women's rights activists say Uruguay has been able to move ahead because of the long separation of religion and government.

"Uruguay has been a secular state for over 100 years, since its construction, and the idea of the secular state is very well integrated in society," said Lilián Abracinskas, the director of the pro-choice NGO Mujer y Salud (Woman and Health). "It is also part of the education system. This is a big difference in comparison with the other countries in the region."

Political activism and collaboration has also been important. Verónica Pérez, a political scientist at the University of the Republic, attributed the passage of the law to the campaigns of feminist activists and their close ties to the left-wing parties that controlled parliament and the presidency in 2012. Other left-wing governments in the region have not been as supportive of women's rights.

"The new Latin American left aren't necessarily secular and this is an obstacle to decriminalisation," she said. "The Uruguayan

process is matched only by the decriminalisation of abortion in the Federal District of Mexico in 2007, where the same combination of factors was present."

Opposition led by Catholic groups has faltered. In 2013, an attempt to overturn decriminalisation through a referendum secured the support of only 9% of voters.

Pérez said free, legal abortion was one of the reasons why Uruguay had the lowest rate of maternal death in Latin America.

Even before the law was changed, the Government had relaxed penalties to enable women to initiate non-surgical abortions at home using drugs. Before that, there were an estimated 20,000 hospital admissions a year because of hazardous, illegal abortions.

## Rest of world

Abortion laws in Australia vary depending on the state in which a woman resides. There is a lack of routinely collected national abortion statistics.

Abortion is either prohibited altogether or is legal only where a woman's life is in danger in many parts of Africa.

The Center for Reproductive Rights maintains a database of abortion laws worldwide which can be viewed at www.worldabortionlaws.com.

* This article was edited on 12 January 2016 to clarify the abortion laws in the United States.

5 January 2016

⇨ The above information is reprinted with kind permission from The Guardian. Please visit www.theguardian.com for further information.

© 2016 Guardian News and Media Limited

# Abortion controversy: pro-choice and pro-life

**Y**ou may have heard lots of information about abortions. Some may have been positive and in favour of them whereas others may have been strongly against them. There is often news of protests going on outside abortion clinics and women feeling intimidated to attend them. Some people believe that you have a right to choose what happens to you while others believe that your foetus or unborn child has the right to life and that should not be taken away from it.

### The pro-choice abortion argument

Pro-choice campaigners aim to ensure that women have the right to choose whether or not to continue with a pregnancy. They believe that the Abortion Act 1967 should be modernised and that safe, legal abortions should be made readily available to all women as and when they need it.

Your right to choose what you do is imperative to these groups and they feel that the law should be changed to reflect this, removing the need for a doctor to assess you to determine your need for an abortion. They also believe that abortions provided through the NHS can be restrictive and quite often are delayed.

Pro-choice groups are trying to get the current law brought in line with the majority of current public opinion and the main areas of focus are:

⇨ Around three quarters of British people believe that you should be able to make your own decision about having an abortion

⇨ To remove the need for a doctor to assess you in line with the current laws and approve your abortion request

⇨ To extend the law to women in Northern Ireland so they no longer have to travel to access abortion services

⇨ To reduce NHS waiting times and make the delay between your appointment and abortion no more than three weeks no matter which NHS Trust you go through.

### The pro-life abortion argument

Pro-life campaigners aim to protect the right to life from conception, through life to then having a natural death. They believe that all life, including that of a foetus, is precious and should not be ended.

Your pregnancy, your foetus primarily, is important to these groups and they place great significance on the development of it deeming abortion "unjust and discriminatory".

While they are completely for your right to choose what you do with your own body and whether or not you have sexual intercourse they are firmly against your right to choose an abortion. There are also groups that do not believe in abortion due to religious beliefs.

You should try not to be swayed by opinions other than your own and, while this can be difficult, if you find out the information for yourself you can then make an informed decision that is right for you.

⇨ The above information is reprinted with kind permission from UK Health Centre. Please visit www.healthcentre.org.uk for further information.

*© UK Health Centre 2015*

# Post-abortion stress – the psychological stress some women suffer after abortion

*By Julia Acott – CareConfidential*

### What is post-abortion stress?

While we would be the first to agree that not all abortions cause obvious distress to all women, nevertheless there are a substantial number who do struggle afterwards. Research has shown that up to 50% of post-abortive women may need antidepressants at some stage in their lives, which they often relate back to problems following the abortion.

Abortion can affect women and some men in the following areas: physically, emotionally, psychologically, behaviourally and spiritually. Post-abortion stress is now recognised as a medical condition.

### The facts

A new study entitled 'Late-Term Elective Abortion and Susceptibility to Posttraumatic Stress Symptoms' has been published in the *Journal of Pregnancy* by Dr Priscilla Coleman of Bowling Green State University in the US and two other colleagues. This is the first ever study to detail the experiences of women having early abortions (up to 12 weeks) compared to those having late abortions (13 weeks onwards). 52% of the early abortion group and 67% of the late abortion group met the American Psychological Association's criteria for Post-Traumatic Stress Disorder (PTSD) symptoms.

### External pressure

The results show breakdowns of whether partners desired the pregnancy, and if there was pressure to abort from people other than partners. In both sets of data, women faced high levels of external pressure, but in later pregnancy they faced particularly high pressure (47.8% compared to 30.5%).

Sadly, nearly 40% of women in the survey said they wanted the baby and fewer than 14% said they received adequate pre-abortion counselling or information on alternatives or the physical and emotional risks.

### The cost to women

Although these read as 'just figures', each of these statistics represents a woman who has suffered a terrible injury as a mother. The right of women to be protected during their pregnancy is being compromised in the name of choice.

Rebecca Ng from the ProLife Alliance comments that when women are at their most vulnerable and should be supported, it is terrible that so many are pressured in this way. It is small wonder that they suffer long-term psychological problems. The ProLife Alliance joins the authors of the study in calling for more counselling and support for women considering abortion at any stage.

### Coping after an abortion

Many women initially feel relieved after an abortion. Some feel sadness about the abortion, but over time cope with it in a way that's acceptable to them.

However, there are some who do not cope well and who experience

various symptoms, which are sometimes called post-abortion stress.

## Symptoms of post-abortion stress (PAS)

Symptoms can include the following:

⇨ emotions such as guilt, grief, sense of loss and anger

⇨ feeling the need to 'replace' the pregnancy

⇨ a feeling of distance from existing children

⇨ inability to maintain normal routine

⇨ depressed feelings, which are stronger than 'a little sadness'

⇨ sleeping problems

⇨ flashbacks

⇨ tearfulness

⇨ disturbing dreams or nightmares

⇨ difficulty being near babies or pregnant women.

In severe cases a woman can become suicidal, self-harming, indulge in risk-taking behaviours, become dependent on drugs or alcohol, suffer anxiety or panic attacks.

## Onset of symptoms

These symptoms can occur at any stage after an abortion and are sometimes triggered by another loss later on.

Some women are more susceptible to these symptoms, particularly if there was uncertainty or ambivalence surrounding the decision.

## Other factors

Other factors that can influence PAS include:

⇨ whether the woman was comfortable with the idea of abortion

⇨ strong motherly feelings or maternal instinct

⇨ previous depression or mental ill health

⇨ feeling she had no choice because circumstances were overwhelming

⇨ having an abortion after a disability had been diagnosed in a wanted pregnancy

⇨ feeling pressurised by someone close.

If you are experiencing any of these please do see your GP.

## Other help

Other help is available – The Journey, a therapeutic programme developed by CareConfidential, enables women to work towards recovery from a troubled abortion experience. This counselling is open to women who are experiencing distress following abortion, whether immediately after or many years later.

If you have had an abortion and need to discuss your feelings with someone please contact CareConfidential for free and in confidence on 0800 028 2228 or visit www.careconfidential.com.

## Crisis pregnancy help

www.careconfidential.com

CareConfidential Helpline

Impartial and confidential:

0800 028 2228

⇨ The above information is reprinted with kind permission from Mental Healthy. Please visit www.mentalhealthy.co.uk for further information.

*© Mental Healthy 2016*

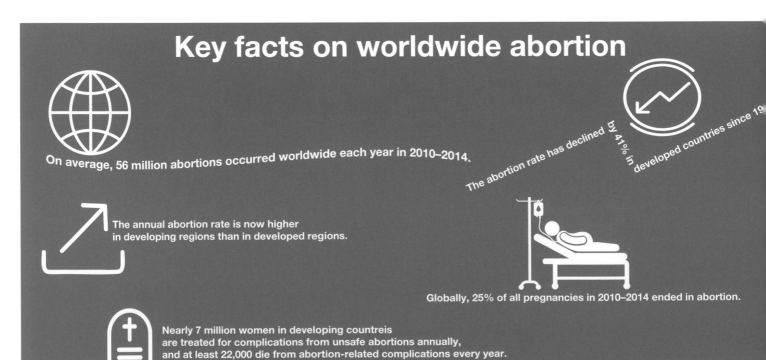

# Key facts on worldwide abortion

On average, 56 million abortions occurred worldwide each year in 2010–2014.

The abortion rate has declined by 41% in developed countries since 19...

The annual abortion rate is now higher in developing regions than in developed regions.

Globally, 25% of all pregnancies in 2010–2014 ended in abortion.

Nearly 7 million women in developing countreis are treated for complications from unsafe abortions annually, and at least 22,000 die from abortion-related complications every year.

*Source: Key facts on induced abortion worldwide, World Health Organization and Guttmacher Institute, May 2...*

# Unplanned pregnancy – the alternatives to abortion

*By Charlotte Fantelli – Mental Healthy and Julia Acott – CareConfidential*

Finding out you are pregnant can be scary, especially if it was not planned. A lot of women in this situation consider abortion, but many of these women are unaware of the alternatives. These are some options you may want to consider if you are facing a 'crisis pregnancy'.

## Fostering

Fostering is not often considered as an alternative to abortion, but there is a lot to be said for having this help in some situations.

Some women may find they need a little time to make changes in their lives in order to become suitable parents. It may be that they need extra help to find appropriate housing or financial support. It may be that they do not want an abortion but need time to decide if adoption is the right path for them and their baby.

Fostering involves the social services, who will place the child with suitable foster parents for a period of up to six months. This can give women vital time, the time they need to sort out obstacles with the help of social services.

It is a myth that social services are child snatchers who take children from loving parents. There is nothing more wonderful than enabling parents to care for their own children, and equipping them with the support they need to do this is one of the roles social services plays.

During this time the mother (and father if appropriate) will be encouraged to access the child and bond as much as possible with the intention of creating a stable environment for that child to enter as soon as it is possible for this to happen.

## Adoption

There are many preconceived ideas about adoption and many myths that cause great concern amongst women who find themselves in an unwanted pregnancy situation. You may think adoption will prohibit you from having children living at home in the future, or that social services will be involved in your future pregnancies, deeming you an unfit parent.

This is simply not the case. There are also more open adoptions taking place, meaning some contact can still be made by the birth parents if appropriate.

### What is the adoption procedure?

When you are ready, a social worker will visit you to talk about it. You don't need to decide now. You have plenty of time to find out what's best for you and your baby.

The baby goes to foster parents for about six weeks. You can visit during this time to be sure that you are making the right decision. The baby then goes to live with the adoptive family. After three months with them, the adoption order can go through.

You do not have to go to court – a social worker will visit you and ask you to sign a legal document. You can still change your mind after the baby's born at any time until the adoption order is made.

## Keeping the baby with you

For women who choose to keep their babies in difficult situations, there is limited support, and it is largely down to the mother to source the support she needs. My own local pregnancy crisis centre Alternatives (see www.altel.org.uk – affiliated to CareConfidential) gives considerable support in such situations, far more than the NHS and social services who frequently refer their clients to Alternatives. The abortion providers have no support services for those who choose not to abort.

### Crisis pregnancy help

www.careconfidential.com

CareConfidential Helpline

Impartial and confidential:

0800 028 2228

⇨ The above information is reprinted with kind permission from Mental Healthy. Please visit www.mentalhealthy.co.uk for further information.

# Position statement from The Royal College of Midwives

**The RCM believes that:**

⇨ Every woman should have control over her own body and her fertility.

⇨ Every woman should have the right to exercise choice over all aspects of her maternity care, including whether to have a baby or not.

⇨ Abortion procedures should be regulated in the same way as all other procedures relating to women's healthcare.

⇨ Every woman has the right to be given the necessary information to make an informed choice regarding her decision as to continuation of the pregnancy or not.

⇨ Every woman has the right to be given the necessary information to make an informed choice regarding the opportunities provided within the law to terminate pregnancy.

⇨ It is within the scope of midwifery practice in the UK for midwives to work with women who are considering whether to terminate their pregnancy and who have made the decision to terminate their pregnancy.

Midwifery practice must always comply with the legal framework relevant to the provision of such services.

⇨ All midwives should be prepared to care for women before and after a termination in a maternity unit under obstetric care.

⇨ The rights of midwives or maternity support workers to hold a position of conscientious objection, as described in the 1967 Abortion Act, should be recognised but should only apply to direct involvement in the procedure of terminating pregnancy.

⇨ Access to safe abortion services is a fundamental healthcare issue for women wherever they live.

⇨ Women who are citizens of the UK should have equitable access to all aspects of reproductive healthcare. Accordingly, the provision of abortion services in Northern Ireland should be brought into line with the rest of the UK.

*Published in 2016*

⇨ The above information is reprinted with kind permission from The Royal College of Midwives. Please visit www.rcm.org.uk for further information.

# Midwives lose case over right to refuse to supervise terminations

*By Steve Ford*

Two Catholic midwives have been told they do not have the right to avoid supervising other nurses involved in caring for patients having pregnancy terminations.

As conscientious objectors on religious grounds, Mary Doogan and Connie Wood had challenged whether their health board could require them to delegate, supervise and support staff who were involved in carrying out terminations.

The Supreme Court in London yesterday ruled against the pair, who had previously won an appeal case in Scotland over their role as labour ward co-ordinators at the Southern General Hospital in Glasgow.

The Royal College of Midwives (RCM) described the new ruling a "sensible decision" that would bring "clarity" to health professionals in similar situations.

Gillian Smith, RCM director for Scotland, said: "The ruling gives extensive definition to complex clinical and other situations, in regard to whether conscientious objection applies or not. Midwives and other clinicians will benefit from this ruling's clarity."

The two midwives believed their right to conscientious objection was breached by being asked to answer telephone calls to book women in and delegate or supervise staff providing terminations to women primarily ending a pregnancy after a diagnosis of foetal anomaly.

A Scottish court ruled in 2013 that Ms Doogan and Ms Wood should indeed have legal protection from such tasks.

However, their employer NHS Greater Glasgow and Clyde appealed, saying the right to abstain should only extend to treatment ending a pregnancy.

The case centred on interpretation of the 1967 Abortion Act, which includes a clause allowing healthcare professionals to refuse to participate in abortion care, provided it is not an emergency.

The Supreme Court judges said parliament was likely to have envisaged that right to refuse as being restricted to "actually taking part".

Lady Hale, deputy president of the court, explained this by saying that MPs would not have viewed it as including managers, administrators, caterers or cleaners involved in running the service.

"The managerial and supervisory tasks carried out by the labour ward co-ordinators are closer to these roles than they are to the role of providing the treatment which brings about the termination of the pregnancy," she said.

" 'Participate' in my view means taking part in a 'hands-on' capacity," she stated.

The RCM and British Pregnancy Advisory Service welcomed the judgement, which they described as a "landmark".

They warned that the previous ruling would have allowed for a widely expanded interpretation of conscientious objection that could have "seriously jeopardised" care in hospitals around the UK.

Such a "broad and unprecedented" interpretation of conscientious objection would effectively have enabled a "tiny number of staff opposed to abortion to make women's care undeliverable in many NHS settings," they argued.

*18 December 2014*

⇨ The above information is reprinted with kind permission from *Nursing Times*. Please visit www.nursingtimes.net for further information.

# Unsafe abortion: seven million women at risk from dangerous pregnancy termination

Unsafe abortions result in seven million women needing treatment for complications every year. Pakistan was found to have the highest rate for women needing medical care following unsafe procedures, a study published in *BJOG: An International Journal of Obstetrics & Gynaecology* found.

Unsafe abortions are one of the leading causes of maternal mortality across the globe, accounting for up to 15% of the 800 women who die from preventable pregnancy-related causes every day. Yet these figures do not take into account the number of women who are left in need of hospital treatment, often leading to lifelong health problems and disability.

Dr Susheela Singh, from the Guttmacher Institute and lead author of the study, said: "We already know that around 22 million unsafe abortions take place each year, resulting in the death of at least 22,000 women. Our study provides further evidence about the number of women who suffer injury as a result of complications due to unsafe abortion, often leading to chronic disability. These statistics represent only part of the problem as they do not include women who need care, but do not visit health facilities."

Most unsafe abortions take place where the procedure is illegal, or in developing countries where well-trained medical practitioners are unaffordable or not readily available. They also take place in areas where modern contraceptives are unavailable. Methods include drinking toxic fluids like turpentine or bleach, inflicting direct injury to the vagina, such as inserting a coat hanger or twig into the uterus, or carrying out external injury like blunt trauma to the abdomen.

The latest study showed Pakistan (where abortion is legal only to preserve the mother's health) to have the highest rate of complications from unsafe abortions, with 14.6 in every 1,000 women aged between 15 and 44 needing treatment. Regionally, Asia had the highest rate, with 4.6 in 1,000 women needing treatment every year. This, the authors said, was driven by high rates in South-Central Asia.

Africa was found to be the next worst region, with 1.6 million women needing care, followed by Latin America and the Caribbean. The lowest treatment rate was found in Brazil, with 2.4 per 1,000 women requiring care. Researchers used official health statistics and studies from 26 countries, and data were adjusted to take into account the number of women receiving treatment in the private sector, and excluding those who needed treatment following a miscarriage.

As well as the huge health burden, the study found unsafe abortions cost an estimated $232 million (£148 million) on post-abortion care in the developing world. Singh said: "The provision of better reproductive healthcare, including access to family planning services, contraception and safe abortion where the law allows, would have significant economic benefits as well as improving the health and well-being of women and their families."

*19 August 2015*

⇨ The above information is reprinted with kind permission from *International Business Times*. Please visit www.ibtimes.co.uk for further information.

# Why are feminist drones dropping abortion pills on Poland?

**An article from The Conversation.**

THE CONVERSATION

*By Anne-Marie Kramer, Lecturer, Faculty of Social Sciences, University of Nottingham*

A Dutch feminist pro-choice activist organisation, Women on Waves, has been using a drone to drop abortion pills across the Polish-German border.

The aim of the flight has been to highlight Poland's restrictive abortion laws – a consistent topic of debate since the fall of communism in 1989.

Abortion was available virtually on demand in Poland between 1956 and 1989. Under state socialism, difficult living conditions or a difficult personal situation were grounds for termination. But in 1993, the country's comparatively liberal abortion laws were comprehensively overturned. With post-communism came one of the most restrictive abortion laws in Europe.

There have been numerous heated parliamentary debates since then, as well as repeated opinion polling and many demonstrations that have seen both pro-life and pro-choice groups calling for changes to the law.

## Restrictive laws

Abortion is only legally permissible in Poland under certain strict conditions. If the pregnancy constitutes a threat to the life or health of a woman, if prenatal examination indicates heavy, irreversible damage of the embryo or if an incurable illness threatening the embryo's viability, it is legal. It is also legal if there is justified suspicion that the pregnancy is the result of an illegal act – but that must be confirmed by a prosecutor.

The law was briefly liberalised in 1996 to allow for abortions on social grounds until the 12th week of pregnancy. But after that decision was ruled unconstitutional, the country reverted to its restrictive legislation.

And even though Polish women face greater difficulty than their fellow Europeans in accessing abortion, pro-life movements affiliated with the Roman Catholic Church are still very much mobilised. They want to restrict access to abortion even further.

The basic objective of the 1993 law was to increase the birth rate and to reduce the numbers of abortions carried out. But Poland still has one of the lowest birth rates in Europe. Meanwhile, a 2013 poll found that between a quarter and a third of Polish women had at least one abortion despite the restrictions.

This is echoed by the World Health Organization, which estimates that countries in eastern Europe (including Poland), have among the highest abortion rates in the world.

According to the Federation of Women and Family Planning, between 80,000 and 100,000 Polish women obtain abortions each year. The fact that in 2011 only 669 legal terminations were registered makes it clear that the law is not stopping the procedures from being carried out.

## Underground abortion

Polish women obtain abortions through a variety of routes. One is via the so-called white coat abortion underground, which can be easily accessed through newspaper adverts promising to "restore menstruation" or provide "gynaecological support – full range".

Such services are unregulated and costly – the price is estimated to exceed the average monthly wage. Given that helping a women obtain an abortion is an offence punishable by imprisonment of up to three years, these services must also be kept secret.

The second major route is via abortion tourism to Germany, the Czech Republic, The Netherlands, Austria, Great Britain and Slovakia. However, as well as the cost of travel, such procedures can cost hundreds of euros.

That's where the drones come in. The third major route is through medical abortion, or so-called abortion pills. Foreign websites such as the one run by Women on Waves, and Women on Web, offer assistance to women seeking abortion. There is also a growing unregulated market in abortion pills on the Internet.

## Not for everyone

Obtaining an abortion via all these methods is contingent upon having enough money to be able to pay – which means poorer women are more adversely affected by the 1993 law.

There is also considerable evidence that access to abortion, even where it is permissible, is very difficult to obtain. To avoid falling foul of the restrictive laws, doctors in Poland routinely avoid or refuse to perform abortion procedures. They often insist on additional certificates, referrals or letters of approval from supervisors, or use the conscience clause to refuse access.

This means that even women who are legally eligible for abortions still continue to use the abortion underground, because obtaining an abortion through the legal channels is so difficult.

While women of childbearing age who have the financial means to do so continue to find ways to access abortion, Polish society remains polarised on the subject.

Initiatives such as the drone missions are but the latest in a long line of attempts to highlight how unjust the system is in Poland, and how the country continues to violate women's rights.

*1 July 2015*

⇨ The above information is reprinted with kind permission from *The Conversation*. Please visit www.theconversation.com for further information.

# Zika emergency pushes women to challenge Brazil's abortion law

**Women's groups are set to challenge the law in the hope of making termination possible for women at risk of delivering a baby born with Zika-related defects.**

*By Sarah Boseley*

Women's groups in Brazil are set to challenge the abortion laws this summer in the hope of making a safe and legal termination possible for women at risk of delivering a baby born with defects after exposure to the Zika virus.

"Women should be able to decide and have the means to terminate pregnancies because they are facing serious risks of having babies with microcephaly and also suffering huge mental distress during their pregnancies. They should not be forced to carry on their pregnancies under the circumstances," said Beatriz Galli, a lawyer on bioethics and human rights who works for Ipas, a group dedicated to ending unsafe abortion.

Lawyers for the organisations will present a legal challenge at the supreme court in the first week of August, when the court sits again after the winter break. They are co-ordinated by Anis Instituto de Bioética, which campaigns for women's equality and reproductive rights.

The groups have obtained an opinion from lawyers at Yale University in the US, who argue that the Brazilian government's policies on Zika and microcephaly have breached women's human rights. The government "has failed to enact adequate measures to ensure that all women have access to comprehensive reproductive health information and options, as required by Brazil's public health and human rights commitments", says a review from the Global Health Justice Partnership, which is a joint initiative of the Yale Law School and the Yale School of Public Health.

It is also critical of Brazil's handling of the epidemic. Its "failure to ensure adequate infrastructure, public health resources and mosquito control programmes in certain areas has greatly exacerbated the Zika and Zika-related microcephaly epidemics, particularly among poor women of racial minorities", the review says.

As of 7 July, there have been 1,638 cases of reported microcephaly – an abnormally small head – and other brain defects in Brazil, according to the World Health Organisation. Women who do not want to continue their pregnancy because they have been infected, even if they have had a scan confirming brain defects in the baby, are unable to choose a legal termination. There is evidence of a rise in early abortions using pills obtainable online and fears that unsafe, illegal abortions will be rising too.

Galli said there were already about 200,000 hospitalisations of women who have undergone a clandestine termination every year, and a suspected 1 million illegal abortions before the epidemic. "We know that there are clinics operating in the very low-income poor settings in Rio and women are paying a lot of money and are risking their lives," she said.

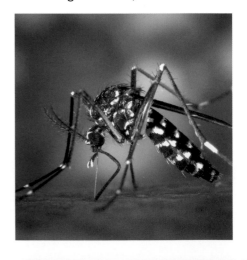

Campaigners who want to change the law are encouraged by a ruling the supreme court handed down in the case of babies with anencephaly in 2012. This is a condition where the foetus develops without a brain, making it impossible for the baby to be born alive. The case took eight years, but eventually the court voted eight to two in favour of making abortion legal in those circumstances.

Before the ruling, there were two exceptions to the ban on termination in Brazil – when the pregnant woman's life was at risk and when she had been raped. Anencephaly became the third, but campaigners acknowledge that it is not a simple precedent.

Debora Diniz, co-founder of Anis and professor of law at the University of Brasilia, said she was confident the court would understand that the situation is an emergency. They were not asking for the legalisation of abortion, she said, but "to have the right to abortion in the case of Zika infection during the epidemic".

"It is not an abortion in the case of foetal malformation. It is the right to abortion in case of being infected by the Zika virus, suffering mental stress because you have this horrible situation and so few answers on how to plan and have a safe pregnancy," she said.

Campaigners have five demands: good information for women in pregnancy, improvements in access to family planning, giving women mosquito repellents, better social policies to help children born with birth defects because of Zika and financial support for parents.

Diniz points out that the worst hit are the poor. "The feeling in my well-to-do neighbourhood [in Brasilia] is that everything is fine," she said. People have never met a woman with Zika or seen a baby with neurological defects. But when she goes to clinics in hard-hit areas such as Campina Grande in the north-east, everything revolves around Zika.

"We have two countries in one country," she said. "This is an emergency of unknown women. The trouble is they were unknown before the epidemic. I'm not being an opportunist. We have an epidemic and the epidemic shows the face of Brazilian inequality."

*19 July 2016*

⇨ The above information is reprinted with kind permission from *The Guardian*. Please visit www.theguardian.com for further information.

# Why it is time to decriminalise abortion

This week the British Pregnancy Advisory Service launched the We Trust Women campaign to remove abortion from the criminal law across the UK. We believe it is both absurd and offensive that in the 21st century a woman in this country could be imprisoned for ending her pregnancy without the legal authorisation of two doctors under legislation passed before women could vote. We want the removal of sections 58 and 59 of the Offences Against the Person Act, which call for a woman who induces her own miscarriage to face life imprisonment, alongside anyone who assists her. Our campaign is supported by many women's organisations, including the Royal College of Midwives, the Fawcett Society, the Family Planning Association and the Women's Equality Party.

The 1967 act did not remove those offending sections of the OAPA; rather, it stipulated that a woman would not be prosecuted if two doctors agreed she met certain conditions. That act was pioneering and profoundly important – yet it was not the triumph of the women's rights movement as it is often perceived to be, but a response to the growing public health problem of backstreet abortions. It placed decision-making firmly in the hands of doctors as to whether a woman would suffer as a result of continuing her pregnancy, painting women's agency almost completely out of the picture.

Decriminalising abortion would change everything – and nothing. It would not increase the number of women needing abortion services or the gestation at which they are carried out, as has been shown in countries where abortion has been decriminalised. Abortion is already tightly regulated in the same way as other healthcare procedures, with staff bound by professional guidelines. This has nothing to do with abortion law.

But it would reflect much more accurately the way in which we see women today. It would put women needing abortion care on the same legal footing as any person requiring medical care – not asking for permission to make a decision about their own body but in partnership with their care provider. As a film to accompany the campaign highlights, it would be a marker of just how far women have come since 1861.

And there are important practical improvements that decriminalisation would bring. The law has held back clinical improvements in care that have benefitted women in other countries, in particular the ability to use certain medications at home for early terminations after they have been prescribed by a doctor – as is recommended by the World Health Organization. We also know the threat of prosecution that is unique to abortion puts doctors off entering this field of women's healthcare. On a regular basis, pregnant women with complex medical needs whose health conditions mean they must be treated in a hospital setting rather than a community clinic are compelled to continue an unwanted pregnancy because they cannot find doctors willing or able to help them. These pregnancies can put their health seriously at risk.

Prosecutions under the OAPA are happening. Just before Christmas, a young mother from County Durham was jailed for two-and-a-half years for inducing her pregnancy in the third trimester using pills obtained online. Later abortions may raise particular moral concerns for many people, but the imprisonment of women should equally so. We know that even women well within the legal limit are obtaining abortion pills online. They may be young women too scared to tell their parents, they may be victims of domestic violence who worry their partner will find out if they visit a clinic. They may also be women who do not know how to access abortion services, or are unable to do so because of their asylum status. The accessibility of this medication means the risk of women breaking the law is now greater than at any point since 1967.

We may question whether these women would be handed the life sentence that can accompany unlawful abortion. But that is beside the point. If we do not think women should go to prison for ending their own pregnancy we should not accept a law that says they should. Taking abortion out of the criminal law will not lead to more women taking their own health into their hands in this way. But decriminalising this procedure – which has enabled women to live their lives as they see fit and bear their children at the time they think is right – would acknowledge and help destigmatise the experience of the one in three women who will need an abortion in their lifetimes. Please support the We Trust Women campaign today.

*12 February 2016*

⇨ The above information is reprinted with kind permission from Progress. Please visit www.progressonline.org.uk for further information.

# Legal abortion until term?

UK abortion provider BPAS has launched a campaign to legalise abortion-on-demand, up-to-birth, for any reason. Parliament is considering debating the issue. For more information on this see http://www.righttolife.org.uk/comment-opinion/abortion-up-to-birth/

The following are my own personal reflections:

My daughter was born at 27 weeks gestational age. She came unexpectedly early, weighed just 2lbs and looked very fragile. Yet she was perfectly formed, alive and a fighter from the beginning. I remember her tiny fingers strongly holding onto my index finger. She had a good thick crop of hair, dark eyelashes, and over the next two weeks she would look at me with an intense gaze, responding physically to sound and to touch. She remained in hospital for eight weeks until she was well enough to come home. By then she weighed 4lbs, but to us she looked huge! She is now 18 and a beautiful, resilient and determined girl. She has had mild asthma throughout her life and missed a fair bit of schooling through colds and chest infections, but that hasn't stopped her from achieving and living a full life and is about to start university.

We had a repeat episode in neonatal intensive care when six years later our son was born. At 26 weeks, he was even a week earlier than our daughter. Like her, he has developed and grown well and is very healthy.

There has been no known reason for my premature labours. I wouldn't wish on anyone the emotional rollercoaster of the first few weeks of being a parent of a premature baby, but it did place my husband and I in a unique position to view (and for many, many hours!) first hand the development of a baby from 26 weeks, which is normally unseen in the womb.

It is one thing to read objectively that the unborn baby is capable of hearing, feeling pain and sensory stimuli. As early as seven to ten weeks, a baby's moves are developed including hiccupping, frowning, squinting, furrowing the brow, pursing the lips, moving individual arms and legs, head turning, touching the face, breathing (without air), stretching, opening the mouth, yawning and sucking. At six months baby will be able to hear, and he or she nestles in her favourite positions to sleep, and stretches upon waking up.[1]

It was incredible to witness this development of a pre-termer first hand. Speak to any mother of a premature baby born after 22 weeks – they will tell you that it isn't an unfeeling foetus that they've given birth to; it is a unique, sensitive and responsive baby, already a 'person'.

Which is why the upper time limit of our country's abortion law, the cut-off point when an abortion is legally allowed to be carried out, already falls too high, at 24 weeks. Seven in ten women want a lower time limit for abortion, as more and more babies born before 24 weeks of gestation survive. A ComRes poll conducted in May 2008 found that 72% of women thought the cut-off point for abortion should be earlier in light of improved survival rates among babies born at a stage when they could legally have been aborted. 73% of women said that the limit should be lowered to 20 weeks or below, given that the limit is no more than 12 weeks in most other EU countries.[2]

It is also why I was particularly concerned to read The Telegraph's article this week[3] about the 'We Trust Women' campaign. The premise is that women know what's best for themselves and shouldn't face prosecution if they self-induce abortion of their unborn child, even through third trimester up until term.

The article states: "The British Pregnancy Advisory Service (BPAS) has now launched a campaign to finally decriminalise abortion in the UK so the procedure can be regulated in the same way as all other women's healthcare."

Now I am a feminist. I believe that women should be allowed the same rights, power and opportunities as men. I am also an advocate of women's rights and of equality, especially in healthcare.

But abortion is often not the best healthcare for women. Arguments for curbing the availability of abortion are supported by mounting evidence that the practice is actually harmful to a woman's physical and emotional wellbeing. In a 2011 study, the largest of its kind and published in the prestigious *British Journal of Psychiatry*, researchers concluded that women having abortions experience an 81% increased risk of mental health problems. It also found almost 10% of all mental health problems in women are shown to be directly linked to abortion. Abortion has also been shown to increase the risk of breast cancer and subsequent premature labours. [4]

Several pro-abortion, women's and feminist groups are backing this campaign.

Royal College of Midwives chief executive Cathy Warwick said it had the RCM's full support. "It is about them (women) having control over their own body and not having their bodies subject to the diktats of others, however well meaning."[5]

I am a nurse, and in the course of my job I meet midwives, both graduates and students, who value the sanctity of life in the unborn baby, and who don't share Cathy's view. They are strongly opposed to legally allowing abortion at whatever stage of pregnancy and I would like to question what consultation the RCM has conducted with its members to voice this opinion and whether it is truly representative of all midwives.

I do not want to belittle the impact and the implications of an unwanted or inconvenient pregnancy, and what is often an extremely challenging and difficult circumstance. Women need maximum support at this time, and the opportunity to have unbiased counselling that includes all possibilities, including adoption. Let's campaign for investment and easier access to tailored support in the common areas of financial stressors, relationship problems, education concerns or parenting challenges that cause many women to choose an abortion.

But this isn't just an issue of woman's healthcare or rights or woman's choice. Another life is involved here. Another life with rights to protect, and let's remember that 50% of these unborn babies are females. I, like many, believe in the intrinsic worth of every human being regardless of race, religion, gender or ability, from womb to tomb.

The advocates of the We Trust Women campaign call the current legislation against women aborting "cruel and archaic".

It's certainly not cruel to the voiceless and defenceless unborn child it protects.

Sources

1. Carlson, B. Human Embryology & Developmental Biology, Toronto: Mosby Publication; 3rd edition, 2004; Tsiaras, A. and Werth, B., From Conception to Birth, a Life Unfolds, New York: Doubleday, 2002.

2. http://www.un.org/esa/ population/publications/ abortion/profiles.htm

3. http://www.telegraph.co.uk/ women/life/womens-charities-call-to-end-cruel-abortion-laws-in-the-uk/

4. http://bjp.rcpsych.org/ content/199/3/180

5. https://www.rcm.org.uk/news-views-and-analysis/news/ campaign-launched-to-remove-abortion-form-criminal-law

*25 February 2016*

⇨ The above information is reprinted with kind permission from CMF Blogs. Please visit www.cmfblog.org.uk for further information.

# Royal College of Midwives backs abortion up to birth

The head of The Royal College of Midwives (RCM) has come under stinging criticism from MPs and pro-life campaigners after she signed up to a campaign seeking to decriminalise abortion.

The RCM released an updated statement on abortion last week and said it supported a campaign being run by bpas (British Pregnancy Advisory Service) which wants to allow abortion right up until birth.

**"To propose abortion up to birth for any reason at all is, I believe, completely out of step both with the society and many of society's representatives in Parliament. We need to stand against this"**

But Cathy Warwick is now facing mounting pressure to resign from her post after it emerged that she failed to consult members and also failed to mention her decision to the board of the RCM.

The *Daily Mail* also reported that as well as being Chief Executive of the RCM, Professor Warwick is also Chairman of bpas, prompting the Head of the Christian Medical Fellowship, Dr Peter Saunders to call for her to resign.

MPs from across the House of Commons also expressed outrage at the RCM's support for abortion right up until birth.

Fiona Bruce MP, Chair of the All Party Parliamentary Pro-life Group told the *Mail*: "To propose abortion up to birth for any reason at all is, I believe, completely out of step both with the society and many of society's representatives in Parliament. We need to stand against this."

Labour MP Rob Flello said: "I am utterly and completely appalled by this abhorrent proposal. This wasn't a minor policy shift by the Royal College of Midwives, it was a fundamental change and the reason they didn't ask their members is because they knew they wouldn't get it past them."

Jim Shannon, DUP MP added: "I will ask the Secretary of State for Health what discussions he has had, or will have, with the RCM and bpas. My concern is that scrapping the 24-week cut-off would be absolutely disgraceful."

James Mildred, spokesman for CARE told the *Mail*: "What sort of message does the RCM's radical stance on abortion send to pro-life midwives? It is tragic."

A new campaign called Not in Our Name has been set up and the website allows you to sign an open letter to Cathy Warwick if you are a midwife or sign a public petition if you are a member of the public.

*17 May 2016*

⇨ The above information is reprinted with kind permission from CARE. Please visit www.care.org.uk for further information.

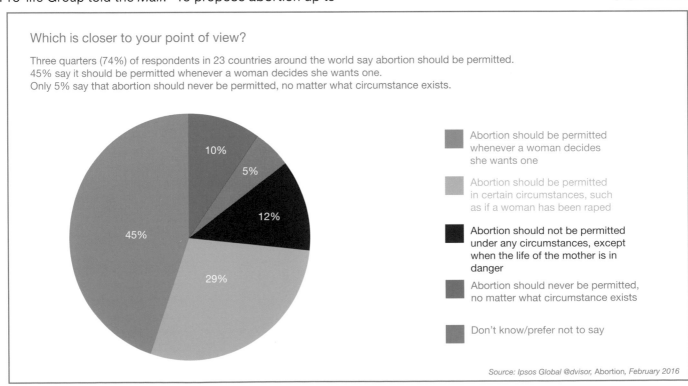

Which is closer to your point of view?

Three quarters (74%) of respondents in 23 countries around the world say abortion should be permitted.
45% say it should be permitted whenever a woman decides she wants one.
Only 5% say that abortion should never be permitted, no matter what circumstance exists.

- 10%
- 5%
- 12%
- 45%
- 29%

Abortion should be permitted whenever a woman decides she wants one

Abortion should be permitted in certain circumstances, such as if a woman has been raped

Abortion should not be permitted under any circumstances, except when the life of the mother is in danger

Abortion should never be permitted, no matter what circumstance exists

Don't know/prefer not to say

*Source: Ipsos Global @dvisor, Abortion, February 2016*

# Midwife slams Royal College of Midwives' support for dropping legal time limit for abortions

**"It is hard to see how there could not be a conflict of interest."**

*By Louise Ridley*

A midwife who was at the centre of a high-profile court case has called on colleagues to "forcefully refuse" to back the "horror" position adopted by their professional body to scrap the time limit for abortions.

Mary Doogan, from Glasgow, took a case to the UK's highest court over whether the right of 'conscientious objection' to the procedure extended beyond participation in actual medical or surgical termination, The Press Association reported.

She has now criticised the Royal College of Midwives (RCM) after its chief executive Professor Cathy Warwick backed a campaign by the British Pregnancy Advisory Service (bpas) calling for abortion to be removed from criminal law.

As Professor Warwick also chairs the bpas board of trustees, Ms Doogan insisted there was a "conflict of interest" at the heart of the "gruesome decision".

Under current laws, a woman can be liable to life imprisonment if she terminates her pregnancy beyond 24 weeks without medical legal authorisation.

In February, the professor, in her capacity as head of the RCM, said the bpas campaign had the union's full support as she called for the legal limit to be 'relegated to history'.

Ms Doogan said: "The professional trade union body, which has the role of representing the vast majority of midwives, has taken the remarkable step of endorsing a campaign which is radically at odds with a positive regard for the babies that midwives work so hard to bring safely into the world.

"The British Pregnancy Advisory Service makes a profit from abortion as a private provider and is calling for abortion to birth to be decriminalised.

"Its chairman is Professor Cathy Warwick, who happens to be the chief executive of the Royal College of Midwives and she has reportedly signed midwives up to the gruesome plan of bpas.

"It is hard to see how there could not be a conflict of interest."

Ms Doogan and colleague Connie Wood took a legal case concerning their rights not to have any involvement in terminations to the UK Supreme Court in London.

While they had no direct role in the procedure, they took the action because they did not wish to book in patients, allocate staff in the ward or supervise and support midwives who care for women undergoing abortions.

They lost their case when Supreme Court justices found participating in treatment meant taking part in a 'hands-on capacity', overturning a previous ruling in their favour by a court in Scotland which declared the right to 'conscientious objection' under the Abortion Act 1967 extended beyond participation in the medical or surgical procedure.

Ms Doogan said: "I entered the profession to bring life into the world not to end life. This is really unbelievable. An unbelievable decision taken in the name of the majority of midwives.

"I would hope that the horror of this position and what is now being demanded of all midwives would penetrate minds and hearts and make them stand up and forcefully refuse to take part in this and oppose this policy decision."

Professor Warwick has already stated RCM members did not require to be consulted over the organisation's support for the bpas campaign.

Earlier this week, she said: "Linking up with this campaign to change the way we provide abortion is totally compatible with the RCM's objective to ensure high-quality healthcare and choice for women.

'We haven't consulted the members and under the way the RCM operates, we don't need to consult our members.

'At the moment we have had very, very significant support from our members on this position, as well as of course a few members who say this is not a position they support."

Under UK law, an abortion can usually only be carried out during the first 24 weeks of pregnancy as long as certain criteria are met.

The Abortion Act 1967 covers England, Scotland and Wales, but not Northern Ireland. The law states that abortions must be carried out in a hospital or a specialist licensed clinic and two doctors must agree that an abortion would cause less damage to a woman's physical or mental health than continuing with the pregnancy.

There are special circumstances which would allow abortion after 24 weeks, such as if there is a substantial risk to the woman's life or serious foetal abnormalities.

*22 May 2016*

⇨ The above information is reprinted with kind permission from The Huffington Post UK. Please visit www.huffingtonpost.co.uk for further information.

# Why we need to clarify our abortion laws

**Despite the official line, our woefully out-of-date Abortion Act is being routinely abused.**

*By Dominic Grieve*

In 2010, Lord Bingham – one of our great jurists – published an important work. In it he sets out what have quickly become known among lawyers as "Bingham's eight principles" – the key ingredients of the rule of law.

Topping Bingham's list is the requirement for the law to be accessible, intelligible, clear and predictable.

When the law is failing to meet these criteria, it should be revised.

It is worth bearing this in mind when examining the law surrounding abortion on the grounds of gender selection.

In my view, the Government is correct when it says: "Abortion on the grounds of gender alone is illegal."

However, the former Director of Public Prosecutions Keir Starmer was also correct when he said: "The law does not in terms expressly prohibit gender-specific abortions."

And the British Pregnancy Advisory Service (bpas) was arguably also correct when it said: "The act does not prohibit a doctor from authorising an abortion where a woman has referenced the sex of her foetus."

The reason that these seemingly contradictory statements are all possible simultaneously is that there is no explicit statement about gender-selective abortion in UK law.

Parliamentarians behind the Abortion Act, 1967, can hardly be blamed for this. Ultrasound was not in common use back then. It never occurred to MPs that anyone would seek to have an abortion because they simply did not want a child of a particular gender.

So how, if there is no explicit prohibition in law, can the Government be correct when it says that the practice is illegal? In a nutshell, because the 1967 act permits abortion only where two doctors form the opinion that the reason for the termination meets the grounds set out in the act. And the gender of the foetus is not one of those grounds.

By far the most commonly cited ground for abortion is that the continuance of the pregnancy would risk greater damage to the mental or physical health of the mother than termination. This is what most people call the "social clause", which accounts for around 98 per cent of abortions – typically around 180,000 a year. Anyone performing or procuring an abortion on any ground other than those set out in the 1967 Act is vulnerable to prosecution under section 58 of the Offences Against the Person Act, 1861 for "procuring a miscarriage".

The problem is that – in some cases – the grounds for abortion under the 1967 act have been turned into little more than a rubber stamp for abortion on demand. Some argue that this ought to be the mother's right, but it is not what the 1967 act allows. If that is what is wanted, we need a new law.

It is quite clear that the "wrong gender" of the child alone cannot fit within the criteria for permitting abortion under the 1967 Act. But the law is being abused. In my view, this presents a powerful case for trying to clarify the law. This presumably is why Parliament voted so overwhelmingly in favour of a motion suggesting precisely that back in November, and this is why I put my name to the amendment that Parliament will consider today.

The amendment is designed to make explicit the current situation in law. It achieves its purpose and does so proportionately. But it is not without controversy.

Some campaigners are vehemently opposed. They are entitled to their view, but it must be said that some of the criticism is founded upon misrepresentation of the amendment's purpose and likely effect.

One commonly held, yet mistaken, view is that this amendment

"criminalises women". The truth is that the amendment does not even apply to women. Rather, it relates to those who apply the grounds of the 1967 Abortion Act – a privilege granted only to doctors.

Another criticism is that this amendment will prevent a woman from accessing abortion where there is a gender-linked disability in the child. This also is wrong.

Currently, doctors can and do conclude that a foetus is at risk of being disabled by establishing the gender of the baby. In certain cases, this may provide a legal justification for abortion.

However, these abortions are not undertaken on the "grounds of the sex of the unborn child". Rather they are undertaken because there is a "substantial risk that the child, if born, would suffer from such physical or mental abnormalities as to be seriously handicapped", as the rather outdated language of the Abortion Act has it.

It is very easy to be drawn into a technical discussion about the law and to forget the reality that this amendment seeks to address. There are women in the United Kingdom who are opting to have gender-selective abortions. If we think that this is in the public interest then we should bring in a new law and sweep away the protections for the unborn child in the 1967 act and accept that there is an entitlement to gender selection by abortion. But we should not allow the present law to limp on in this state any longer. For these reasons, I would urge all colleagues in the House to support the amendment today.

* Dominic Grieve MP, was Attorney General from 2010–2014.

*23 February 2015*

⇨ The above information is reprinted with kind permission from *The Telegraph*. Please visit www.telegraph.co.uk for further information.

# Why I oppose a ban on sex-selection abortion

**An article from The Conversation.**

*By Pam Lowe, Senior Lecturer in Sociology, Aston University*

THE CONVERSATION

A campaign is underway in the UK to make it illegal to abort a child based on its gender. Proponents say they are worried about women being coerced into terminating female foetuses and that action needs to be taken to stop discrimination against baby girls.

But this is a flawed argument. You cannot promote gender equality by enacting laws that place restrictions on women's bodies. Banning sex-selective abortion opens up a world in which there is such thing as a "good" and "bad" reason for an abortion. What's more, it implies coercion is a reproductive health issue rather than what it actually is – an act of domestic violence.

## The truth about abortion law

The campaign to ban sex-selective abortions is currently focused on getting an amendment into the Serious Crime Bill. Conservative MP Fiona Bruce has tabled an amendment to the bill which has the support of more than 70 other members of parliament who want to see it fast tracked into legislation in the next few months.

Contrary to popular belief, abortion is still a crime in the UK. The 1967 Abortion Act did not repeal earlier legislation that criminalised abortion. It does not give women the legal right to an abortion. Instead it provides a legal defence for the crime of abortion if the conditions of the act are met. Within the act, abortion was framed as a health issue and the legal defence of abortion is based on the health implications of pregnancy for both the woman and foetus.

So, for example, abortion will comply with the act if, in the clinical judgement of two doctors, continuing the pregnancy will pose a greater risk to a woman's physical and mental health than if she terminated.

The act does not list any specific reasons, such as rape, where this might be the case. It therefore avoids setting up a list dictating the circumstances under which an abortion is "good" or "bad".

Categorising abortion by acceptable or unacceptable reasons needs to be avoided. As the evidence from elsewhere shows this can lead to simplistic judgements about women's lives and behaviour. It might be agreed that being raped is a "good" reason for abortion, for example, but then there would need to be a mechanism to prove a rape took place.

Making abortion a health issue in the law also means that the decision is a matter between women and doctors. The views of their partners or wider families cannot be considered. Introducing a specific ban on sex-selection abortion will change this. Doctors would have to investigate family life in order to rule out this motive, eroding women's privacy. This is not progress towards ending discrimination against women.

## Restricting abortion

The main force behind the campaign to ban sex-selection abortion are members of the Pro-Life All-Party Parliamentary Group – of which Bruce is the chairwoman. Like all anti-abortion groups, its mission is to end abortion, not to promote women's rights. In the UK, the majority of the population supports legal abortion, so rather than directly challenge abortion, pro-life groups seek alternative ways to restrict it.

This strategy is widely used in the US, putting onerous regulations on abortion providers that make running abortion services more difficult. This has led to clinics closing. Pro-life groups have successfully blocked access to abortions without having to directly ban abortion itself.

The same tactic is now clearly being used in the UK. If campaigners can restrict abortion for this reason, they will simply move to the next.

### Domestic violence

Women being coerced into terminating a pregnancy on the basis of the foetus's sex is a serious issue. But we need to be clear that this is not a reproductive health issue, it is domestic violence.

In many cases, women living with this form of domestic violence will simply not disclose that foetal sex is the reason for the abortion. No doctor can legally carry out an abortion if a woman has not given her consent, so if a woman did disclose coercion it could not take place. Banning sex-selective abortion is highly unlikely to be the solution to this problem.

The supporters of this ban suggest that outlawing sex-selective abortion is sending an important message to specific communities that it is wrong to discriminate against baby girls. Yet it will do nothing to really help.

Although it may seem counter-intuitive, supporters of women's rights need to oppose the banning of sex-selective abortion. This campaign has nothing to do with ending gender discrimination. It is a strategy of the pro-life movement to reduce women's access to abortion more generally. While the continuing discrimination against women which leads to coercive abortion for gender reasons is a serious problem, you cannot end gender oppression by placing new restrictions on women's lives.

*26 January 2015*

⇨ The above information is reprinted with kind permission from *The Conversation*. Please visit www.theconversation.com for further information.

# Pro-life group: Scotland will become abortion tourist destination if termination laws are changed

A pro-life group has claimed that Scotland will become an abortion tourist destination if the laws around termination are changed.

The Don't Stop A Beating Heart campaign, which opposes any extension to the current UK termination laws, made the claim as it raised concerns over plans to devolve abortion legislation to Holyrood.

Campaigners have urged Nicola Sturgeon to use the new powers to decriminalise abortion. However, the First Minister has said she has no plans to amend the laws around terminations.

A new campaign, called We Trust Women, has now been launched by the British Pregnancy Advisory Service, calling for the current legislation to be changed. It has been backed by groups including the Royal College of Midwives, Fawcett Society, Maternity Action and End Violence Against Women.

A spokeswoman for Don't Stop A Beating Heart said: "The reality is that women are often pressurised to have an abortion – abolishing abortion law will mean more pressure on women in Scotland to submit to abortion, and less real support for pregnant mothers.

"Already, well in advance of the transfer of legislative authority, we are hearing a clamour for further extension of the existing excessively liberal law. This could

No!
Thou shalt not ...
or at least
not here!

see abortion legalised from the existing 24-week limit, in most cases, up until the point of birth.

## "If we keep going at the current annual pace of abortion, then in less than three years Scotland will reach the 500,000 mark since the passing of the Abortion Act in 1967"

"That's why pro-life supporters from different backgrounds, people of faith and none, in addition to concerned organisations and individuals have decided that we must stand together in the face of this onslaught.

"In their statement, the abortion lobby call for 'Woman centred care' – but abortion is a traumatic and damaging procedure, carrying physical and mental health risks for women."

The campaign group claimed that 8.5 million abortions have taken place in the UK since 1967, with 11,475 occurring in Scotland.

## "The reality is that women are often pressurised to have an abortion – abolishing abortion law will mean more pressure on women in Scotland to submit to abortion, and less real support for pregnant mothers"

The campaign's spokeswoman added: "If we keep going at the current annual pace of abortion, then in less than three years Scotland will reach the 500,000 mark since the passing of the Abortion Act in 1967.

"If the law is liberalised that total will be reached much sooner, fuelled by women travelling from all over the UK and beyond to make use of the relaxing of the laws.

"That would be a tragedy for every unborn baby whose life

is taken. It would also be a tragedy for this country if its reputation throughout the world is to be sullied as we become known as an abortion tourist destination."

Scottish ministers are due to get control over abortion laws as part of the Scotland Bill, which is currently going through Westminster.

Labour has said that it will try to delay the devolution of abortion by a year to allow time for a review into the potential consequences.

Under the 1967 act it is illegal for a woman to have an abortion without the permission of two doctors. However, campaigners want this law changed so that the permission of only one doctor is required.

Ann Furedi, the chief executive of bpas, told the *Herald*: "Scotland has a proud tradition of progressive abortion policy and practice, and devolution provides the Scottish Government with the opportunity to once again lead the way.

"One in three women will have an abortion in their lifetime in the UK.

"The ability to end a pregnancy has enabled women to live their lives in the way that they see fit and bear children at the time they think is right.

"It is high time we recognised this by taking abortion out of the criminal law, and making clear that we trust women to make their own decisions about their own lives and bodies."

**Abortion should be permitted whenever a woman decides she wants one**

| Country | % |
|---|---|
| Sweden | 84% |
| France | 69% |
| Great Britain | 62% |
| Hungary | 62% |
| Turkey | 60% |
| Spain | 59% |
| Canada | 57% |
| Belgium | 56% |
| Italy | 55% |
| Australia | 53% |
| Germany | 50% |
| Russia | 45% |
| US | 41% |
| India | 40% |
| Japan | 35% |
| Poland | 33% |
| South Korea | 32% |
| South Africa | 31% |
| Argentina | 26% |
| China | 26% |
| Mexico | 25% |
| Brazil | 16% |
| Peru | 11% |

*Source: Ipsos Global @dvisor, Abortion, February 2016*

A Scottish Government spokeswoman said it has no plans to change the law on abortion, adding: "Abortion is provided to all women in Scotland who require it, within the law."

*9 February 2016*

⇨ The above information is reprinted with kind permission from *Herald Scotland*. Please visit www.heraldscotland.com for further information

*© Herald Scotland 2016*

# Six outrageous facts about abortion in Ireland

*By Shiromi Pinto*

The fight for safe and legal access to abortion in Ireland is on. Here are six facts that bring home the true impact of Ireland's draconian abortion law.

### 1. In Ireland, abortion is only allowed if you are in danger of dying

Abortion is banned except where there is a risk to your life – but not health. The definition of "risk" is narrow and vague. So it's almost impossible to actually have an abortion in Ireland.

### 2. Breaking Ireland's abortion law could get you 14 years in jail or a €4,000 fine.

If you have an illegal abortion in Ireland, you risk 14 years in prison. If you're a healthcare provider and refer a woman to seek an abortion abroad, it's a fine of up to €4,000. Ireland's abortion law criminalises women, girls and the healthcare professionals who try to help them.

### 3. A woman must carry to full term a foetus that won't live

If a woman is carrying a foetus that is unlikely to survive, she must still carry that pregnancy to term under Irish law. The trauma of doing this is summed up by Amnesty International's Grainne Teggart: "How cruel would it be to make me go through this… To put me through a full pregnancy. I would have the breast milk, I would have everybody asking me how long are you gone?... How could they think that would not affect someone mentally?"

### 4. Equal right to life. Not equal in practice

The 8th Amendment to Ireland's Constitution, made in 1983, protects the right to life of the foetus and places it on an equal footing with the right to life of the woman. Most of the women and health professionals Amnesty spoke to, said that a woman's rights inevitably come second. Lupe, a woman who was forced to carry a dead foetus for two months, told us: "When a woman gets pregnant in Ireland, she loses her human rights."

### 5. Ireland is happy for you to have an abortion – as long as it's not in Ireland

Under Irish law, it's legal to travel abroad to get an abortion, prompting the criticism that Ireland is happy to export its human rights responsibilities. Emma Kitson, who went to the UK for an abortion because her foetus had a fatal medical condition, said: "We deserved to have support within the Irish healthcare system, to get us through that... They export the problem and they forget all about you."

### 6. Each year, about 4,000 women and girls leave Ireland to have an abortion in the UK

Many feel like criminals for doing this. As Cerys, who travelled to the UK for an abortion, put it: "I am a law-abiding citizen and I felt like I was committing a crime, like I was smuggling drugs across the border. That feeling was horrible."

A woman seeking an abortion is a woman trying to get the healthcare she needs. She is #notacriminal. Tell Ireland to change its abortion law. Sign our petition today.

My Body My Rights is Amnesty's global campaign for sexual and reproductive rights.

*9 June 2015*

⇨ The above information is reprinted with kind permission from Amnesty International. Please visit www.amnesty.org for further information.

# How Northern Ireland could be forced to ditch its "nightmare" law

**This week sees a landmark court case, as Northern Ireland's Human Rights Commission and Amnesty come together to try and change the "harshest criminal abortion law in Europe". Méabh Ritchie reports.**

*By Méabh Ritchie*

If you are raped in Northern Ireland, you can't legally get an abortion.

If you're a 13-year-old sex crime victim in Northern Ireland, even of incest, you can't legally get an abortion.

If you are pregnant and find out, after a 20-week scan, that the foetus you're carrying has a serious abnormality and will soon die in your womb, you can't legally get an abortion.

Last week the British media rightly rallied around a report condemning abortion laws in the Republic of Ireland. But right here in a corner of the UK, unlawful abortion still carries a life sentence both for the woman undergoing it and for anyone assisting her.

It is only legal if a woman can prove her life – physical or mental – is at risk.

These strict restrictions mean that just 23 terminations were carried out at NHS hospitals in Northern Ireland last year. An estimated 4,000 women were forced to leave Ireland, north and south, to terminate their pregnancy, with an estimated 2,000 travelling to England.

Many more women order 'illegal' abortion pills from sites such as Women on Web.

But this law could be about to change – not through politics, despite a recent government consultation on this issue – but through the courts.

Today, a High Court Judicial Review will examine a case brought by Northern Ireland's Human Rights Commission against the Department of Justice.

Over three days, the commission will make the case for a change in the law to allow the termination of pregnancy in circumstances of rape, incest or complications which will result in the death of the foetus.

## 'Inequity' in the UK

Amnesty Northern Ireland has taken the unprecedented step of intervening to support the commission against the law, which it says carries the "harshest criminal penalties in Europe".

"It's a dire situation," says Amnesty's Grainne Teggert. "It's inequity in the UK.

"Politicians are beginning to change their mindset, but that's no good. We need the words of politicians to become actions and legislate for change. Women can't afford to wait."

It has also become more urgent following an English High Court judge ruling in May 2014 that an 18-year-old woman from Northern Ireland was not entitled to a 'free NHS abortion' in an English hospital. The case caused huge controversy and the girl and her mother are currently appealing the High Court decision.

The impact of the north of Ireland's highly restrictive abortion law is something that Sarah Ewart, 24, who is also submitting evidence to the High Court review, knows only too well.

## "A living nightmare"

In October 2013, she found out 20 weeks into a much-wanted pregnancy that her baby had anencephaly, a fatal abnormality where the brain does not develop and has no skull.

The only option doctors in Belfast could offer her was continuing with the pregnancy until the foetus died and then inducing a painful labour.

Doctors couldn't even give any advice about where to seek alternative treatment, for fear of being jailed. She was forced to travel to London to have the pregnancy terminated.

"I am an ordinary woman who suffered a very personal family tragedy, which the law in Northern Ireland turned into a living nightmare," she said.

In the midst of her ordeal, Ms Ewart, phoned a BBC Radio Ulster show to explain her devastating predicament, and in doing so shone a light on the impact of these restrictive laws.

"I was grieving, I was losing the baby but it was something I felt passionately about," she told me.

Before 2013, Ms Ewart was opposed to abortion, "but this baby I was carrying – there was no chance of life. This kind of situation hadn't crossed my mind."

Now, she is campaigning for a change in the law on abortion.

There is an active pro-life lobby in Northern Ireland within both the Catholic and Presbyterian communities, but Ms Ewart's story was universally recognised as grossly unfair.

When she visited a private clinic with her husband to try and find out about other options, she was confronted by the aggressive protesters who stand vigil outside, waving blood-red placards of foetuses.

"Pro-life protesters were shouting all sorts, flashing cards in my face," she recalls. "We were trying to get into my granny and granddad's car and we couldn't open the door."

But after the radio interview, the wider public has been much more sympathetic: "Now if we're in town or something, people stop us, they say they're behind us."

## Sea change of opinion

Sarah Ewart's experience of public opinion appears to be backed up by recent polling. Around 65 per cent of people surveyed by Amnesty last year in Northern Ireland believed that abortion should be made available in certain circumstances.

This is by no means a mandate for abortion on demand. But it is still a sea change, says Amnesty's Grainne Teggert, and an acknowledgement that abortion is not a black and white, "pro or anti" issue.

"For years, no one talked about it," says Jenny McEneaney of the Belfast Feminist Network, "but people are talking about abortion now.

"Being anti-choice is the default in Northern Ireland. But when you have those conversations, you start to see people changing their minds."

Politicians have been slow to reflect this change in opinion through policy. The justice department held a consultation into fatal foetal abnormality, in light of Ms Ewart's story, and recommended that abortion should be made legal in this case.

But the DUP, Northern Ireland's largest party, and the nationalist SDLP are still vehemently pro-life and reluctant to be seen to make any concessions.

Despite being very sympathetic to Ms Ewart at the time, First Minister Peter Robinson of the DUP has since backtracked and said that the law doesn't need to be changed.

Instead he offered to publish long-awaited guidance on the existing law, despite a previous DUP health minister, Edwin Poots, acknowledging in 2013: "any changes around lethal foetal abnormalities would require amendments to criminal law."

In fact, just two weeks ago, the DUP tried to increase the criminal penalty for abortion and close down the Marie Stopes clinic. The motion was outvoted by just 41 to 39.

After a year of lobbying politicians, this is why Amnesty is supporting legal action, echoing the landmark 1973 Roe vs Wade case that legalised abortion for the first time in the United States.

"Sometimes when you need radical social change – and this is radical for Northern Ireland – it's usually through the courts that it has to happen," adds Ms McEneaney.

"There's no way that it'll pass through the (government) Assembly."

All eyes will be on Belfast's High Court next week, and a judgement is expected after the judicial summer recess. It won't change things overnight, but a ruling in favour of the Human Rights Commission would give women the option of getting around the law, as the court could compel a health trust to assist with a termination.

But for Ms Ewart? This is personal.

"For some people this is a political debate," she said, "but for me, this is my life."

*15 June 2015*

⇨ The above information is reprinted with kind permission from *The Telegraph*. Please visit www.telegraph.co.uk for further information.

# Don't Screen Us Out initiative to protect babies with Down's

Don't Screen Us Out, a campaign highlighting concerns over the proposed use of a new prenatal test for Down's syndrome, was launched last week.

The new test uses NIPT (non-invasive prenatal testing) to screen a pregnant mother's blood for tiny fragments of DNA.

These fragments (cell-free DNA) are then checked for abnormalities, including Down's syndrome, or trisomy 21. The screening is offered between 11 and 14 weeks of pregnancy.

The Don't Screen Us Out campaign, led by international advocacy group Saving Down Syndrome, warns that the new test will "enable a kind of informal eugenics in which certain kinds of disabled people are effectively 'screened out' of the population before they are even born".

### More lives lost

The UK National Screening Committee (UK NSC) has recommended that the new screening procedure, also called the cfDNA test, be added into the NHS Fetal Anomaly Screening Programme.

The test is touted as a safer option than amniocentesis, which is the current test recommended to women who have a one in 150 or greater chance of having a baby with Down's syndrome. Unlike cfDNA testing, amniocentesis carries with it the risk of miscarriage.

But critics of cfDNA testing point out that more children will be found to have Down's using this new method, which will lead to more babies' lives being lost. Currently, nine out of ten babies who test positive for Down's syndrome are aborted.

In a response to the UK NSC's consultation on cfDNA screening published last October, Christian Concern highlighted that this new procedure could lead to an additional 92 abortions on the basis of a Down's syndrome diagnosis every year.

### New campaign highlights dangers

Don't Screen Us Out encourages people to ask their MPs to oppose the new cfDNA screening process, which will enable an "informal eugenics" in British society.

The UNESCO International Bioethics Committee has also issued a strong warning on the ethical implications of approving such a test. The committee's report states:

"A widespread use of NIPT, namely as general screening in order to detect abnormalities, followed by an abortion, is perceived by some people as an evidence of the will to avoid permanent pain in a lifetime, by others as a sign of a situation of the exclusion society gives to people affected by this illness, meaning indirectly that certain lives are worth living, and others less."

The same report says that there is no way to ensure that this technique, which would also provide information on the gender of the child at an earlier stage in pregnancy, would not be used for "gender-abortion".

### "All lives valued"

People with Down's syndrome can lead happy and fulfilling lives, and many are making unique contributions to society. An American woman with Down's syndrome runs a non-profit to encourage full inclusion of people with Down's syndrome, and an Australian teenager with Down's is pursuing a career as a model.

Andrea Williams, Christian Concern's Chief Executive, said: "It is shocking that our health service will be further facilitating abortion on the basis of disability. Babies with Down's syndrome are created in God's image and their lives are infinitely valuable to him – and ought to be treasured by us."

*17 January 2016*

⇨ The above information is reprinted with kind permission from Christian Concern. Please visit www.christianconcern.com for further information.

# Abortion: why aren't men allowed to have a say?

**The state assembly of Ohio has tabled a bill which would give fathers a final say in abortion. Isn't it time men were given a voice in such important matters, asks Neil Lyndon.**

While an electoral earthquake shakes the very foundations of the political establishment across Europe, a faint tremor is being felt, far way, under the tectonic plates of an implacable order that has held power across the developed world for the last 50 years.

In the state assembly of Ohio a bill has been tabled which would give fathers a final say in abortion. Their written consent would have to be obtained before an abortion could be effected. If a father refused consent, the abortion would not be allowed.

So far as I know (and this subject has been on my mind for over 25 years), this is the first time since the development of abortion by vacuum curettage in the 1960s – and David Steele's Abortion Act of 1967, which made that simple, safe technology available to all women under the NHS – that any legislature has given consideration to the possibility that a man who has effected a pregnancy ought to be accorded a voice in its termination. Up until now, men's views and feelings on this issue have been absolutely inadmissible; and where any man has tried to raise his voice he will have been denounced – as I have been – as an enemy of "a woman's inalienable right to choose".

According to one of its co-sponsors, the Ohio bill is based on the principle that "since fathers will have legal responsibilities for child support, they should have rights regarding the birth or destruction of the foetus".

Under the terms of the bill, if the woman said she has no idea who might be the father, she would be required to provide a list of names of men who might conceivably fit that bill. Those men would then have to be tested in order to establish the identity of the father and that individual would be required to give written

permission before the abortion could be performed. If the father cannot be identified, the woman would not be allowed to terminate her pregnancy.

Where the woman says that the pregnancy is the result of rape, she would have to provide a police report as evidence before she could have the abortion.

Heavy sanctions would back up these provisions. A woman who forges the signature of an alleged father and a man who falsely claims to be the father in order to help a woman in getting an abortion would both be subject to criminal prosecution – as would the doctor who performs an abortion without the written consent of the father.

Wow! The Ohio bill is, apparently, very unlikely to pass into state law; but even if it is not going to shake our earth it looks, at least, as if it might be a straw in the wind. In its unequivocal radicalism, it eclipses all previous attempts to assert any rights of men in abortion.

I thought I was being daring in my 1992 book *No More Sex War* when I wrote:

"Women who choose to have an abortion might be a good deal better off if their men were required to endorse and support their decision. If the man agrees, the burden of the decision will be shared. If the man does not agree, he ought to be provided with a means to say

so. His opinion ought, at least, to be registered and recorded. I'm not saying it ought to have any restraining force in law. I'm not saying a woman should be prevented from having an abortion if the father disapproves. I'm just saying he has a right to be heard."

These tame suggestions got me hauled over the coals of the feminist orthodoxy on my way to a pelting in the stocks. Not for the first time. When, in 1989, *The Times* published a column of mine in which I mourned the absence of two aborted children whom I might have fathered, the paper received so many letters in response that they had to be run on full half-pages on consecutive days. 19 out of 20 of those correspondents furiously told me that, as a man, I had no right to express any opinion on abortion and I could keep my feelings of loss to myself.

When my book was published, I was summoned to the cellars of Broadcasting House for an inquisition at the hands of that Torquemada of *Woman's Hour*, Jenni Murray. "A woman's rights over her own body must be indisputable," she thundered. "OK," I answered. "But they are not the only rights at issue in a pregnancy" – a proposition which, to my surprise, she seemed to accept without demur.

That's the bottom line. The woman's right to choose is, obviously, not the only concern – despite the fury with

which feminists have been insisting on that position for 50 years.

On top of the highly contentious question whether the foetus in the womb has philosophical, moral and legal rights which place a duty of care on the wider society, the inseminating man must clearly, undeniably have an active interest which ought to be established and recognised with legal rights. And then, too, the wider society which pays for the operation under the NHS in Britain should also save a say. Is it in the interests of taxpayers that 150,000+ abortions should be performed every year? Is it in the interests of the wider society that those lives – more or less equal to the annual figure for net migration in the UK – should be stilled?

Or are those questions only allowed in Ohio?

*28 May 2014*

⇨ The above information is reprinted with kind permission from *The Telegraph*. Please visit www.telegraph.co.uk for further information.

# In the abortion debate, women's voices matter more than men's

*By Catriona Stewart*

For women to have an equal place in society they must have full autonomy over their bodies. That's really the beginning and the end of the debate right there.

But of course, it's not, because there are too many outside factors vying to take a stake in what women choose to do with their bodies and when.

With the proposed devolution of abortion legislation from Westminster to Holyrood in the Scotland bill, there has begun a bout of shadow boxing – of arguments full of ifs, maybes and might bes.

If abortion legislation is devolved then maybe the time limit, currently 24 weeks, will be reduced due to the pressure of Scotland's religious right. If abortion legislation is devolved then maybe this will be the chance for change, thanks to Scotland's progressive left.

Whether devolution will lead to challenges to the current legislation is a wait-and-see issue. However, the voices of those of an anti-abortion stance have not seen fit to wait. I purposefully do not use the expression 'pro-life' – it's not pro the mother's life, is it?

Listening to this topic being debated last week and this, it has been astounding the number of male voices looking to set down their opinions as fact, their opinions being that a foetus should have equal rights to that of the woman gestating it. There was a chap given airtime on the radio this week to say that he's not religious but, re: abortion, we're all going to hell.

Though, it's not that astounding that men should feel it's their place to tell women what to do with their bodies. Parliament is male dominated. It is, in reality, men who make the decisions about women's reproductive choices.

What I wonder about these men who like to shout their opinions about situations that will never affect them is this: why aren't they using that breath to gather the boys together for a bit of a chat? If it's so important to them that a woman carries to term a baby that she does not want, cannot afford and that will alter her life beyond recognition why aren't these same men making the effort to ensure that parental leave is shared equally between men and women? Why aren't they at the head of the queue offering to go part time or give up work to stay at home and look after the children? Why aren't they campaigning for the male pill? Why are they not foster parents?

If all life is sacred, why are they not actively making changes to societal frameworks that allow for thousands of children to live in grinding poverty, day in, day out, with barely hope of change?

Do they choose to use their bodies to sustain life – are they organ donors? Do they regularly give blood? Can I have a kidney, please?

If your viewpoint is that life begins at conception that's fine. It's your viewpoint to hold. But it's not a viewpoint that should be used to turn women into little more than vessels. And it is merely a viewpoint. There is no medical, theological or philosophical agreement on when life begins therefore facts must be used.

The fact is, there will be times that a woman's life is best served by not becoming a mother. Maybe she was raped. Maybe her partner is violent or coercive. Maybe she cannot financially sustain two lives. Maybe it's just not the right time.

Maybe she has agonised over the decision; maybe the decision has given her no pause at all. Maybe she will regret it for the rest of her life; maybe it will be the last thing on her mind.

Where there is no maybe is that it must be her choice.

If men were told they had no right to decide for themselves whether or not to remove a ball of cells from their penises that is, at best, life changing and, at worst, potentially lethal, there would be no conversation to be had.

I wouldn't for a minute suggest that men should hold no view on abortion. But I would hope they could separate the notion that all life brings joy from the fact women have a right to be more than a vessel, whether that is for another human being or for religious ideology or for sentiment.

The devolution of abortion to Scotland has the potential to open up a space for debate but it's women's voices I want to hear, not the scolding of men with nothing to gain and nothing to lose. Men who will raise their voices for an unformed, abstract foetus and not for the experience of the fully formed women in front of them.

*16 November 2015*

⇨ The above information is reprinted with kind permission from *Herald Scotland*. Please visit www.heraldscotland.com for further information

# Key facts

- The Abortion Act 1967 came into effect on 27 April 1968, permitting abortion in Great Britain (not including Northern Ireland) by registered practitioners subject to certain conditions. (page 1)

- The crude abortion rate in 2014 was highest at 28.0 per 1,000 for women aged 20–24. The under-16 abortion rate was 2.5 per 1,000 women and the under-18 rate was 11.1 per 1,000 women, both lower than in 2013. (page 1)

- The majority of abortions are performed at or under 13 weeks gestation.(page 1)

- 32% of abortions in 2014 were performed in NHS hospitals and 67% in NHS agencies, totalling 98% of abortions. The remaining 2% were privately funded. (page 2)

- Among women who have experienced a previous abortion 27% are under 25 and 46% are over 25. (page 2)

- If you pay for an abortion at a private clinic, the cost is around £400 or more – depending on the stage of your pregnancy. (page 4)

- By law, two doctors have to agree that you can have an abortion. Usually this is the first doctor you see and a second doctor who will perform the abortion. (page 5)

- 37% of the abortions carried out under ground E (substantial risk that if the child were born it would suffer from such physical or mental abnormalities as to be seriously handicapped) in 2015 were because of chromosomal abnormalities. 22% were because of congenital malformations of the nervous system. (page 7)

- The abortion rate for England and Wales was 15.9 per 1,000 women aged 15–44 in 2014. Rates fell slightly among all age groups under 25, and remained stable or rose marginally among women over 25. 56% of abortions in England and Wales were performed on women over the age of 25 in 2014. (page 10)

- In 2014, nearly 4,000 abortions were conducted in private clinics, with costs ranging from £600 to over £2,000. (page 11)

- In Finland, Iceland and the UK restrictions are in place yet abortion rates remain relatively high at 174, 223 and 253 terminations per 1,000 live births. (page 14)

- Unsafe abortions are one of the leading causes of maternal mortality across the globe, accounting for up to 15% of the 800 women who die from preventable pregnancy-related causes every day. (page 22)

- A recent study showed Pakistan (where abortion is legal only to preserve the mother's health) to have the highest rate of complications from unsafe abortions, with 14.6 in every 1,000 women aged between 15 and 44 needing treatment. Regionally, Asia had the highest rate, with 4.6 in 1,000 women needing treatment every year. This, the authors said, was driven by high rates in South-Central Asia. (page 22)

- According to the Federation of Women and Family Planning, between 80,000 and 100,000 Polish women obtain abortions each year. The fact that in 2011 only 669 legal terminations were registered makes it clear that the law is not stopping the procedures from being carried out. (page 23)

- Three quarters of respondents in 23 countries around the world say that abortion should be permitted. 45% say it should be permitted whenever a woman decides she wants one and only 5% say that abortion should never be permitted, no matter what the circumstances. (page 28)

- By far the most commonly cited ground for abortion is that the continuance of the pregnancy would risk greater damage to the mental or physical health of the mother than termination. This is what most people call the "social clause", which accounts for around 98 per cent of abortions – typically around 180,000 a year. (page 30)

- 84% of people in Sweden think that a woman should be permitted an abortion whenever she wants one. This is in contrast to 35% in Japan and just 11% in Peru. (page 33)

- If you have an illegal abortion in Ireland, you risk 14 years in prison. If you're a healthcare provider and refer a woman to seek an abortion abroad, it's a fine of up to €4,000. (page 34)

- Strict restrictions mean that just 23 terminations were carried out at NHS hospitals in Northern Ireland last year. An estimated 4,000 women were forced to leave Ireland, north and south, to terminate their pregnancy, with an estimated 2,000 travelling to England. (page 35)

### Abnormality

An abnormal or disformed feature. With unborn babies or foetus's this can refer to a disability or feature which would prevent a child from leading a relatively normal and happy life once it was born, and can, therefore, be a reason to terminate a pregnancy.

### Abortion

A procedure which prematurely ends a pregnancy through the death and expulsion of the foetus. It can occur naturally (spontaneous abortion), but this is more commonly referred to as a miscarriage. The term 'abortion' usually refers to the deliberate termination of an unwanted pregnancy (induced abortion).

### Conception

The act of fertilisation, where an egg (ovum) joins together with a sperm (spermatozoon) to form an embryo or zygote. This term describes the moment a woman becomes pregnant.

### Contraception

Anything which prevents conception, or pregnancy, from taking place. 'Barrier methods', such as condoms, work by stopping sperm from reaching an egg during intercourse and are also effective in preventing sexually transmitted infections (STI's). Hormonal methods such as the contraceptive pill change the way a woman's body works to prevent an egg from being fertilised. Emergency contraception, commonly known as the 'morning-after pill', is used after unprotected sex to prevent a fertilised egg from becoming implanted in the womb.

### Embryo (zygote)

Between day 14 and week eight of pregnancy the fertilised egg is referred to as an embryo. A zygote is simply the scientific term for the fertilised egg which is made by the joining of an egg (ovum) and sperm (spermatozoon). After the eighth week of pregnancy an unborn baby is referred to as a foetus.

### Female infanticide

Infanticide is the unlawful killing of very young children and babies. Female infanticide specifically refers to the practice of killing female babies and young girls and is a practice that has been reported in India, China and parts of Africa, Asia and the Middle East.

### Gestation

The development period of an embryo or foetus between conception and birth. As the exact date of conception in humans can be difficult to identify it is usually dated from the beginning of a woman's previous menstrual period.

### Neonatal

Referring to an unborn child, or the period of time before a child is born.

### Obstetricians and gynaecologists

An Obstetrician or Gynaecologist is a person who specialises in treating diseases of the female reproductive organs.

### Paternalistic

Referring to the act or practice of managing other individuals.

### Pro-choice

Pro-choice supporters believe that it is a woman's right to choose whether or not to continue with a pregnancy. They also believe that the choice to have an abortion should be available to all.

### Pro-life

Pro-life supporters believe that life begins at the moment of conception and think that an unborn child, foetus or embryo has the same rights as any other living person. They believe that the law should be changed so that abortion would be heavily restricted or outlawed in the UK.

### Terminate

A term meaning 'to bring something to an end', an abortion is sometimes referred to as a termination.

### The Abortion Act 1967

This act decriminalised abortion in cases where it had been certified by two doctors that certain grounds had been met, such as a serious risk to the mental or physical health of the pregnant woman.

### Viability

This refers to a foetus's ability to survive outside the womb. In UK law, the 24th week of pregnancy is the point at which the foetus is considered to be viable, and therefore the latest point at which an abortion can be performed. However, some people have argued that this should be reduced as medical advances mean that some premature babies born at 24 weeks, or fewer, are surviving.

# Assignments

⇨ Design a series of social media posts and short video clips that could be used by a pro-choice charity to spread their message.

## Brainstorming

⇨ In small groups, discuss what you know about abortion.

- What is the law regarding abortion in the UK?
- What are some of the reasons a woman might decide to have an abortion?
- What are the names of the two main arguments regarding abortion rights?

## Research

⇨ Research historical attitudes towards abortion in England. Start with the 1800s and work your way back to present day. Make some notes about your findings then share with the rest of your class.

⇨ Research abortion law in a country other than England. Write a short summary and then feedback to your class.

⇨ Conduct an anonymous questionnaire to find out whether people in your year group believe that abortion should be legal or illegal. When you have gathered your results create a graph or pie chart to demonstrate the different percentages.

⇨ Research the 'legal abortion until term' dilemma. What would this involve? Would there be restrictions? What do the Royal College of Midwives think about the subject? Write a bullet point list of what you find out.

⇨ Why has the Zika virus 'pushed' women in Brazil to challenge its abortion laws? Start by reading the article on page 24, then widen your research using the Internet. Use your findings to write a one-page article.

## Design

⇨ Create a leaflet for young women who are considering an abortion. It should give advice about where they can go, who they can talk to, the risks, the alternatives and the practicalities.

⇨ Choose one of the articles from this book and create an illustration that highlights the key themes of the piece.

## Oral

⇨ In small groups, debate whether you think men should be given a say in whether women have abortions.

⇨ Create a PowerPoint presentation that explains the alternatives to abortion.

⇨ In pairs, go through this book and discuss the cartoons you come across. Think about what the artists were trying to portray with each illustration.

⇨ The article on page 21 tells how two Catholic midwives have lost the right to refuse supervising terminations. As a class, debate whether you think midwives should be required to supervise abortions, no matter what their religious views are.

⇨ Stage a debate in which half of your class argues on the side of the pro-life argument and the other argues for pro-choice. Think carefully about the views of your allocated side and try to understand why they believe what they do.

## Reading/writing

⇨ Read the article *Why are feminist drones dropping abortion pills on Poland?* on page 23 and write a summary for your school newspaper.

⇨ Watch the film *Vera Drake*. Write a review explaining whether you think the film is pro-abortion, pro-life or pro-choice? What other messages do you think the film portrays to its audience, and what does the film say about the consequences of abortion?

⇨ Write an article which will explore the following question: 'Why is it important to educate students about contraception, pregnancy and abortion?'

⇨ Write a blog post exposing the truth about abortion law in Ireland. Use the articles in this book to help you.

⇨ Imagine you are an agony aunt. You have received a letter/e-mail from a man who's girlfriend has decided to terminate her pregnancy. The man is very against this decision and wants her to keep the child. What advice would you give?

# Acknowledgements

The publisher is grateful for permission to reproduce the material in this book. While every care has been taken to trace and acknowledge copyright, the publisher tenders its apology for any accidental infringement or where copyright has proved untraceable. The publisher would be pleased to come to a suitable arrangement in any such case with the rightful owner.

## Images

All images courtesy of iStock except page 24: Pixabay.

Icons on page 18: Globe made by MadeByOliver, declining arrow made by Darius Dan, inclining arrow made by Tracy Tam, grave stone made by Freepik and pregnant lady made by Freepik – all for www.flaticon.com.

## Illustrations

Don Hatcher: pages 20 & 32. Simon Kneebone: pages 14 & 23. Angelo Madrid: pages 6 & 34.

## Additional acknowledgements

Editorial on behalf of Independence Educational Publishers by Cara Acred.

With thanks to the Independence team: Mary Chapman, Sandra Dennis, Christina Hughes, Jackie Staines and Jan Sunderland.

Cara Acred

Cambridge

September 2016